CHURCH, CHICAGO-STYLE

WILLIAM L. DROEL

acta
PUBLICATIONS

CHURCH, CHICAGO-STYLE
by William L. Droel
with a Foreword by Patricia Crowley, OSB

Edited by Gregory F. Augustine Pierce
Cover and text design and typesetting by Patricia A. Lynch
Subway map © 2008 Chicago Transit Authority. All rights reserved.
Used with permission.

Published by ACTA Publications, 5559 W. Howard Street, Skokie, IL 60077-2621,
(800) 397-2282, www.actapublications.com

Library of Congress Catalog number: 2008925912

ISBN: 978-0-87946-362-5

Printed in the United States of America by Versa Press

Year 15 14 13 12 11 10 09 08
Printing 15 14 13 12 11 10 9 8 7 6 5 4 3 2 First

CONTENTS

A Note from the Publisher... 7

Foreword by Sister Patricia Crowley, OSB 9

Introduction 13

RUSSELL BARTA 19

The Vision of Vatican II 23

A Theology of Work... 25

Let the Laity Be Laity.. 31

MONSIGNOR JOHN EGAN... 35

Liturgy and Justice: An Unfinished Agenda................................ 39

In Praise of Vatican II 45

FATHER DENNIS GEANEY, OSA.. 49

Hillenbrand and the Shift to Vatican II...................................... 53

Work: A Lost Identity 55

Creators of the World: The Meaning of Work and Vocation....... 57

MONSIGNOR GEORGE HIGGINS.. 61

The Social Mission of the Church.. 65

The Act of Social Justice is Organizing 68

A Warning from Chicago 71

ED MARCINIAK.. 74

Being a Christian in the World of Work....................................... 79

We Need Action... 91

MARY IRENE ZOTTI.. 95

History of the Young Christian Workers...................................... 99

NATIONAL CENTER FOR THE LAITY... 105

A Chicago Declaration of Christian Concern............................. 109

Nine Principles for Lay Initiative 117

Afterword.. 123

Acknowledgments 127

DEDICATION

To Bernice Barta and Virginia Marciniak (d. 1990),
sisters-in-law and models of church,
Chicago-style.

A NOTE FROM THE PUBLISHER

So OK, some of the selections in this book are a little bit dusty. When you read them, however, you will discover (or rediscover, as the case may be) the vibrancy that the Catholic Church can have, and has had, and could have again. There is a sense of urgency and passion and optimism in these pages that we Catholics often don't feel today. Instead we have to listen at Mass to repeated instructions on when to sit, stand or kneel, or the proper posture for receiving communion. Or we find in our Catholic periodicals endless pages on the pros and cons of bringing back the Latin Mass that most of us have no intention of ever attending anyway.

The clergy and lay people presented in *Church, Chicago-style* didn't have time to argue about such trivial things. They were too busy trying to bear fruit in the vineyard, as Jesus urged us to do. These people were "allergic to injustice," as Ed Marciniak used to say. They were people of the Dismissal, who couldn't wait to be sent forth from Mass to help build the kingdom of God, "on earth, as it is in heaven."

My friend Bill Droel is in the direct line of these men and women. He was attracted to move to Chicago because of them, and he has kept their legacy alive more than any other single person through his community involvements, his writings, and his own good example. He is the longtime volunteer editor of *INITIATIVES*, the respected and indispensable newsletter on faith and work published by the National Center for the Laity, and a leader in the Coalition for Ministry in Daily Life. In this book he pulls together some of the seminal writings of the Chicago Catholic church and introduces each writer with personal insight, warmth and humor.

Every publisher markets some books regardless of their doubtful profitability. This is one such book for ACTA Publications. (On the other hand, should it sell tens of thousands of copies, my children can complete their college education.) We published it because it documents a very important time in United States church history and, more importantly, it suggests a way of being and doing church. If young adult Catholics can somehow capture the spirit of this book, then our church would once again be on track in its mission to make the world more like God intends things. If that happens, the church's current preoccupation with internal matters will be put in their proper perspective.

Monsignor Dan Cantwell used to tell seminarians, "Don't get ordained unless you believe in the vocation of the laity." Church, Chicago-style used to believe that. Maybe it can again.

> Gregory F. Augustine Pierce
> President and Co-Publisher
> ACTA Publications
> Chicago, Illinois

FOREWORD

by Patricia Crowley, OSB
Prioress, Benedictine Sisters of Chicago

The book you hold in your hands is an important piece of the kaleidoscope of books and articles recounting the amazing reality of the Catholic Church in Chicago during my youth. Those early years of my life were filled with people who made history in the Catholic Church—in Chicago, in the United States, and in the universal Church. A slide show of that period would include much of what is recounted in this book, and that is thrilling for me to read.

I grew up thinking that everyone in the world knew about the mystical body *(Mystici Corporis)*, the vernacular at Mass, the "observe/judge/act" process as an essential in gospel living, the great labor encyclicals of Pope Leo XIII, and the Rule of Saint Benedict. Then, I realized one day that what I knew as "ordinary" Catholicism through my parents, Pat and Patty Crowley, was indeed "extraordinary" for much of the country. Church life for me was filled with expansive experiences such as welcoming students from other lands to our dining room table or sharing our bedrooms or spending time with other Chicago families whose homes were poorly heated and under-furnished. Our family vacations were spent connecting with Christian Family Movement (CFM) groups in living rooms across the country, or in Combermere, Canada, with "the Baroness" Catherine de Hueck, or with the Trapp Family in Stowe, Vermont.

Church, Chicago-style imbued us with a sense that "we were the church" and that action for social justice was part of and parcel of our very being. Bill Droel's innate love of and dedication to lay leadership in the church bespeaks my own experience of church.

I knew personally some of the people in this book—I taught Russ Barta's daughter and Ed Marciniak's daughters at St. Scholastica Academy in the 60's and 70's. Ed was helpful to me by connecting me to influential Chicagoans when I was trying to raise money for the Howard Area Community Center and for Deborah's Place. Father Dennis Geaney, OSA, was often at our house, and I always loved listening to him at our dining room table. Monsignor Jack Egan was a special friend and mentor. His familiar voice on the phone would often be asking me to meet with a certain young person who had just come to Chicago and wanted to know about homelessness here.

These men were friends of my parents. However, as I read about them, I began to think about the fact that so few women were mentioned in this collection. My own life reflection is filled with memories of great women (my mother, Rose Lucey, Dorothy Drish, Reg Weissert, Dorothy Day, Catherine de Hueck, Ann Harrigan to name a few). In my own religious community, I have known so many great women: Dolores Schorsch, OSB, in education, Cecilai Hinebaugh, OSB, and Mary Louise Lichtenberger, OSB, in liturgy, Laura Walker, OSB, in leadership, Miriam Wilson, OSB, in prison ministry, Mary Benet McKinney, OSB, and Sheila McGuire in inner city education and many others who served quietly and with great strength. The church and society into which I was born was one in which women were active (and influential) but often not seen front and center. Even my mother, who was college-educated and articulate, usually took the role of organizing things and of supporting my father who did a good part of the public speaking for the two of them.

As a child, one "game" we often played in the basement of our suburban home was to "play" Mass. I remember wanting always to be the priest. Early on, however, I realized that role was not really within my reach. The external structure of the church remains male-dominated, but today the strength and courage and creativity of women is evident and becoming stronger and stronger in new ways each year. The church is still alive—even in the sometimes stultified structure of an all male clergy. Perhaps today's Church, Chicago-style can lead the way on this issue as well through Chicago-based organizations such as Call to Action and the National Center for the Laity.

In the Catholic Church women are faced with a new reality. In the past twenty-five years or so, I have been part of burgeoning movements among women, including the National Assembly of Religious Women (N.A.R.W.), the Women's Ordination Conference (W.O.C.), Woman Church Convergence, etc. I have seen women in key roles in the church and in society on all levels. I can easily cite women front and center as writers, dramatists, preachers, pastors, leaders in social change and even, more recently, as ordained (albeit irregularly) priests.

I also find it energizing to participate in the amazing phenomenon of interfaith relations among Jewish, Christian and Muslim women in the Chicagoland area and around the country.

When I was asked to write this Foreword, I thought to myself "Why me?" Then I began to look at the people featured in this book and thought, "This is a splendid glimpse of the world of my childhood." I also thought about the fact that as a person I have, in small ways, lived out the heritage of this particular chapter of Chicago's church history in my many years of putting into action the gospel message that I learned as a child. Saint Scholastica Academy, the Howard Area Community Center, Deborah's Place, and the many people touched by those ministries are all bearing the fruit of that era.

I feel very honored to contribute to this "treasure" of a book, and I highly recommend it to you, its prospective reader.

INTRODUCTION

I n making a case for a Chicago style of Catholic thought and action, generalizations are necessary. Despite newspaper headlines about its divisions, Catholicism, among all worldwide religions, is remarkably unified. Its dogma, liturgy, sacramental system, devotion to Mary, calendar of saints and more is the same north to south, east to west.

On the other hand, there are many accents within Catholicism. For example, some teachings are stressed more in one diocese than another; some hymns that resound in one parish are never used at a neighboring parish; some Catholics are committed to social justice, others think their church is a refuge from a frightening world. The accent in Chicago is unique and strong. It resonates with the city's magnificent architecture, stuffed pizza, garnished hot dogs (no ketchup), machine politics and manic-depressive Northside/Southside baseball. This is not always obvious to those who live in the Windy City (named not after the Lake Michigan breeze but the verbosity of our politicians), but it is certainly so to outsiders (like myself) who either immigrate to Chicago or spend anytime at all studying the Chicago church.

During the late 1960s and early 1970s, like many other Catholics, I became fascinated with the spirit of the Second Vatican Council. Eager to learn the background for the Vatican II changes, I rummaged through some moral theology textbooks and histories of Catholicism, particularly U.S. Catholicism and quickly realized that many of the Vatican II precursors, participants, and promoters had a Chicago pedigree. In 1978, at the age of 29, I moved from Rochester, New York, to Chicago specifically to connect with Catholicism, Chicago-style. I never left.

Upon arriving in Chicago I enrolled in some classes at Mundelein College where, through Sister Carol Frances Jegen, BVM, I was introduced to Russell Barta, a professor at Mundelein College. Through Barta and his wife, Bernice, I met most of the many people associated with Catholic social action in Chicago from the 1930s through the 1970s, starting with Bernice's brother, Ed Marciniak, and Ed's wife, Virginia. In quick succession I came to know personally Monsignors Dan

Cantwell and Jack Egan, Patty Crowley, John and Theresa McDermott, Larry and Jeanne Ragan, Edmund Rooney, Bob and Mary Cronin, Samuel Nolan, Faustin Pipal Sr., Anne Zimmerman, Father Dennis Geaney, OSA, Dick Morrisroe, Vaile and Mary Scott, Peggy Roach, Peter and Betty Foote, Father Larry Kelly, Marty and Patricia Burns, Tom and Kay Gaudette, Arthur Falls, Bruce and Betty Rattenbury, Franklin and Irene McMahon, Tess and Bill Donnelly, Edmund and Evelyn Stephen, Nina Moore, Monsignors John Hayes and Bill Quinn and many more. Through these people, I met other, younger, Chicagoans interested in our Catholic tradition, whose names are too numerous to mention. I was also privileged to meet a few former Chicagoans who had exported the Chicago-style to other cities: Anthony Downs, Sargent Shriver, Mathew Ahmann, Bob Senser, Monsignor George Higgins, and Peter and Peggy Steinfels.

From all these people, I heard stories about Chicago-based organizations like the Catholic Labor Alliance, the Christian Family Movement, the monthly *Work* newspaper, the Catholic Interracial Council, the Cana Conference, John A. Ryan Forum, Saint Benet's Bookshop, the Adult Education Centers, Chicago Inter-Student Catholic Action (CISCA), the Office of Urban Affairs, the Catholic Guild for the Blind, the Council on Working Life, the Catholic Action Federation, the Summer Biblical Institute, the Industrial Areas Foundation, the Childerly Retreat House, the ACTA Foundation, the National Catholic Social Action Conference, the National Conference of Christian Employers and Managers, the Fides Publishers Association, the Sheil School of Social Studies, the Thomas More Association and more. My newfound friends also told me about national organizations that had a strong presence in Chicago, including the Catholic Worker movement, Friendship House, the Catholic Committee on Urban Ministry, Young Christian Workers, Young Christian Students, the Catholic Lawyers Guild, the Catholic Evidence Guild, the National Council of Catholic Nurses, the Association of Catholic Trade Unionists (ACTU), the National Catholic Conference on Interracial Justice, the Catholic Association for International Peace, the Bishops' Committee on Migrant Workers and more.

Obviously, there was great variety among these pioneering organizations and their leaders. A few melodious chords, however, were played fervently and frequently in Chicago. The Chicago brand of social thought and action during the timeframe presented in this book (the 1930s through the 1960s) and exemplified by the people in this book stressed these themes:

- There was an élan about Catholicism's place in the city and the wider world. The understandable defensiveness of immigrant Catholicism was gradually giving way to confidence as Catholics assumed positions of responsibility in business, the professions and civic life. Church, Chicago-style rejected sectarian tendencies or triumphal attitudes. Far from thinking that Catholics were a pure remnant in a hostile culture, the people in this book and their friends were eager to engage the wider culture.

> THE CHICAGO STYLE invited lay leaders to live the gospel on the job, within the family and around the neighborhood, without requiring geographic or congregational affiliation.

- Church, Chicago-style put strong emphasis on lay initiative in collaboration with chaplains and other supportive Church employees. The people in this book sometimes disagreed on precisely how priests and other Church employees should address specific public policies, but they all were clear that the world is the province of the laity and that baptism—not priestly ordination—is what confers a responsibility to promote peace and justice in all Christians.

- Church, Chicago-style complimented parish life with movements and centers having a non-geographical constituency. The movements and centers were not competing with parishes. In fact, many of them used one or another parish church as a base. Simply, the Chicago style invited lay leaders to live the gospel on the job, within the family and around the neighborhood, without requiring geographic or congregational affiliation. It was assumed that each person would belong to a geographical parish. In fact, most Chicago Catholics, then as now, will identify themselves by parish rather than neighborhood name, as in "I'm from Saint Gall's" or "I live in Queen's," (meaning Queen of Martyrs or All Saints, not a borough north of Brooklyn).

- Church, Chicago-style appreciated that liturgy and justice have a reciprocal relationship. There's even a slogan in Chicago: "The liturgy is the second school of social justice." (The family, of course, is the first school.)

- Church, Chicago-style understood that the usual locus for social action is inside one's workplace, not normally through a Church-endorsed lobby group. This was taken for granted. Thus most of the people in this book were chagrined by the post-Vatican II shift from independent lay initiative to institutional Church-as-lobby-group.

- Church, Chicago-style was very devoted to the Eucharist and animated by the image of the mystical body of Christ. That is, Chicago Catholics (even before Vatican II) were as devoted to the real presence of Christ in the Eucharist as they were convinced of the real presence of Christ in their coworkers, their neighbors and the poor.

- Church, Chicago-style recognized that Catholic action in a diverse city demands close collaboration with Protestants, Orthodox Christians, Jews, Muslims and others. During the time profiled in this book, improving race relations was a major agenda item for Chicago Catholic leaders.

- The people in this book and their friends were studiously devoted to papal encyclicals and other Church teaching—with a clear understanding that doctrine is made for men and women, not the reverse. In other words, they were in love with the church's tradition for the sake of applying that wisdom to changing circumstances.

- Along the same lines, Chicago Catholics liked to tell stories about the church's saints and sinners, especially its Chicago characters. The patron saint of Chicago Catholicism might well be Studs Terkel, a Jew, because he exemplifies the Chicago style of theology-by-story-telling.

Most of the movements and organizations from the 1930s through the 1960s were defunct when I arrived in Chicago in 1978. With one or two exceptions, the few still around were on the skids and/or no longer based in Chicago. However, several new groups were emerging in the 1970s—eager to spread the message and excitement of Vatican II.

Since 1978, I've supported or gotten involved with several of Chicago's post-

Vatican II groups (including Call to Action, the Interfaith Committee on Worker Justice, Cursillo, and the multitude of community organizing efforts, some connected with the Industrial Areas Foundation and some not). I am most involved, however, with the National Center for the Laity (NCL), which was founded as a secretariat to the 1977 *Chicago Declaration of Christian Concern* (reprinted in this book). In 1984, my fellow Rochester refugee and friend Greg Pierce took over leadership of the NCL from Russ Barta and Ed Marciniak. It was not a difficult *coup d'etat*, since both Barta and Marciniak were eager for a new generation of leadership for the organization. The NCL, in my opinion, has kept close to its mission of interpreting, protecting and promoting the Chicago Catholic action tradition from the 1930s, through Vatican II and into the 21st century. Therefore, the excerpts in this book were selected to reinforce the NCL ideology (although not everyone in this book was directly associated with the NCL).

> CHURCH, CHICAGO-STYLE was very devoted to the Eucharist and animated by the image of the mystical body of Christ.

The reader will notice that most of the excerpts in this book come from men, several of whom are priests. The exceptions are the NCL documents, written by committees that included important women leaders. I have also included the case study of the Young Christian Workers by Mary Irene Zotti.

I am uncomfortable with a book featuring so many men, even in a book about the past. Women were certainly leaders in Catholic social action in Chicago. For example, Patty Crowley, mother of Sister Patricia Crowley, OSB, who wrote the Foreword to this book, was directly associated with Monsignor Reynold Hillenbrand and clearly a leader in the Chicago church. She, with her husband Patrick and a few other couples, started and long maintained the Christian Family Movement.

The fact is, however, Patty Crowley and other women leaders were not writing Catholic social theology. They were busy making contacts, raising money and implementing programs. The job of writing theology, until recently, went mostly to men and mostly to priests. The situation was only a little more inclusive in New

York City, where Dorothy Dohen, Dorothy Day and others were writing about Catholic social action. Thankfully, things are now changing in Chicago and in the universal church, and I am especially thankful to Pat and Patty Crowley's daughter, Sister Patricia Crowley, OSB, for contributing the Foreword to this book.

Finally, a word about style: The talks and documents herein are lightly edited for inclusiveness. A few historical references have been made to assist recognition. In keeping with the style of the writers, *church* with lower case c is used to mean the people of God church. *Church* with upper case C is used to mean institutional Church. When in doubt, the more inclusive *church* is used.

Welcome to Church, Chicago-style. I know it has something very important to teach us all.

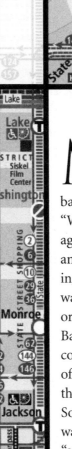

RUSSELL BARTA

1918 - 1997

My telephone would ring during half-time of a Sunday basketball or football game. "We've been attacked," an agitated Russell Barta would announce, even before saying hello. What it all meant was that an article in *America* or *Commonweal* had not, in Barta's opinion, given full consideration to the place of workaday Christians in the church and in the world. Sometimes the phone call was a calmer reference to a "suggestive" or "intriguing" phrase he saw in *America*, *Commonweal*, the *New York Times* or *Newsweek*.

Barta and I were introduced in September 1980 by Sister Carol Frances Jegen, BVM, at Mundelein College (now part of Loyola University, Chicago), where

Barta taught from 1963 until his retirement in 1985. I was a graduate student and Barta was teaching courses like "Church and Society: Models of Involvement," "American Catholic Social Thought," and "Work: Explorations in American Spirituality."

Each class would find Barta rummaging in a battered briefcase for an old article by, for example, Father John Courtney Murray, SJ, on religious vows, or an old retreat manual by Cardinal Stefan Wyszynski of Poland, or a footnote in a 1973 book by Daniel Bell on Christian charity, or a quotation from Simone Weil, Dorothy Sayers or Dorothy Day. Barta would somehow make these obscure references relevant and lead a discussion in class that was sure to continue later over coffee or a beer.

> RUSS BARTA
> was a North American Catholic treasure...in love with the church, a teacher, a mentor and a modern prophet.

Barta was disappointed that North American Catholics were not reflecting on our own experience with liberation but instead were borrowing "images and language" from European and Latin American theology. He wondered why we imported theology from Germany, Holland, France and Latin America. To balance things, Barta was constantly Xeroxing out-of-print material from North American Catholic theologians such as Father Isaac Hecker, CSP, Orestes Brownson, Bishop John Ireland, Father Virgil Michel, OSB, and more.

Liberation theology, first developed in Latin America, was at the time all the rage, Barta noted. Its "hallmark is the priority given to the concrete lived experience of people as reflected in history and culture." Why don't the North American fans of liberation theology reflect on our own "long tradition of democratic practice and social movements that have kept the revolution of 1776 slowly but steadily moving forward"?

Before I met him, Barta already had a long career in education and activism. Born and raised in Berwyn, Illinois, he obtained his bachelor's degree from Saint Mary of the Lake Seminary, his master's degree from Loyola University and his doctorate from the University of Notre Dame. In 1955, he began the Adult

Education Center for the Archdiocese of Chicago. Through that Center, and later at Mundelein College, he brought countless people up to speed with Vatican II. Barta was not only an expert in Catholic philosophy; he gave many Chicago priests their first exposure to historical-critical Scripture scholarship. In fact, during the 1950s and 1960s, the address "21 E. Superior," where Barta and his friends worked, "became synonymous with the confident enthusiasm of Chicago Catholics," writes Father Steven Avella in *This Confident Church* (University of Notre Dame Press, 1992).

Barta's writing usually took the form of lecture notes for hundreds of talks at conferences, summer institutes, public hearings and more. He regularly contributed to *New City*, a twice-monthly Chicago magazine on urban issues that he edited during the 1960s. His research on ethnicity and his opinions on the church appeared in several other magazines and journals. Barta was the founding president of the National Center for the Laity in 1978 and wrote for its newsletter, *INITIATIVES* almost up to his death in 1997.

Russ Barta was a North American Catholic treasure: gracious, slow to criticize, persistent, attentive to detail, in love with the church, a teacher, mentor and a modern prophet.

THE VISION OF VATICAN II
by Russell Barta

Vatican II was a watershed in the church's self-image and attitude toward the world. Unlike a sect that maintains a distance (and thus its purity) from the established centers of culture, commerce, industry and politics, the Catholic Church envisioned by Vatican II is to be at the center of human enterprise, in all its glory and frailty....

The church realizes for the first time at Vatican II that its knowledge of humankind and history and even of the world is only partial. It is no longer a one-way street—the human enterprise coming to the church for guidance. Now the church needs to come to the human enterprise in order that the church can better understand the meaning of revelation....

Vatican II was the first council to take seriously the efforts of ordinary Christians to integrate their faith and their worldly endeavors. It raised this personal and often hidden struggle to the level of public concern and policy for the whole church....

> NOW THE CHURCH needs to come to the human enterprise in order that the church can better understand the meaning of revelation.

Vatican II marveled at the perfection that human work and enterprise had wrought in the world and acknowledged that such labors are religiously significant...

In one of the most poignant sections of Vatican II's *Pastoral Constitution on the Church in the Modern World (Gaudium et Spes),* after recalling again the mastery of modern societies over the whole of nature, the world's bishops put to the church questions reflected in the eyes of modern women and men: "What is the meaning and value of this feverish activity? How should all these things be used? To the achievement of what goal are the strivings of individuals and societies heading?"

In responding to such basic questions of meaning, Vatican II produced the foundation for a worldly spirituality. Vatican II brings together in one unified

Christian vision the God of Creation and the God of Redemption—the *sine qua non* of an authentic Catholic work ethic....

Vatican II's vision of work and creation is exhilarating, powerful. It is a bright light cutting through the fog of the daily routine, the daily grind. But it is a buried treasure. The opening to a unique Catholic worldliness providentially provided by Vatican II desperately needs Catholics to take the initiative on the job, around the home and in the neighborhood.

A THEOLOGY OF WORK
by Russell Barta

I magine a society in which the singular title of honor is that of worker, but worker stripped of its class connotations. In such a society distinctions based on the division of labor are subsumed (thus subordinated), under the title of *worker*. Doctors, corporation executives, lawyers, scientists, academics, as well as machinists and assembly-line operators, would all wear, with pride, the title of worker. In this society such abstractions as technology, progress, culture, science and the arts would be seen for what they essentially are: various forms (or products) of human labor. Work would be perceived as intimately related to the humanizing and spiritual enhancement of the self, yet one's daily work would also be regarded as the normal outlet for service to the community and the practice of other virtues. The workbench, once the exclusive symbol of manual labor, would now serve as the constitutive image of all productive activities.

It is such a radical vision of the place of work in human life which distinguishes Pope John Paul II's 1981 encyclical *On Human Work* and makes it a new and remarkable contribution to the Catholic social tradition. John Paul II envisions a civilization in which the basis of human solidarity rests on the sociological fact that in our time all men and women have become workers.

More than just critiquing the position of work in both socialist and capitalist societies, John Paul II looks to the future and develops a theological understanding of work that could undergird the post-socialist, post-capitalist world. Only once does John Paul II refer to *employers* or *employees*, a distinction so important to socialism and capitalism. For him there are only workers. His celebration of work is not restricted to manual work—an ideological bias found in both socialism and capitalism. Neither is work seen as the basis of a class struggle. On the contrary, it is a basis of human solidarity.

The encyclical *On Human Work*, novel though it be, should be understood as the growing end of an older tradition, much of it buried in the cupboards—a tradition whose basic insight was that we are on the verge of a civilization based on the spirituality of work.

It was Simone Weil who in *The Need for Roots* perhaps first gathered together some loose strands in this tradition and gave it a name: "Our age has its own particular mission or vocation—the creation of a civilization founded upon the spiritual nature of work. The thoughts relating to this vocation…are the only original thoughts of our time, the only ones we haven't borrowed from the Greeks."

> "OUT OF THE CARES,
> toils, duties, afflictions and responsibilities of daily life are to be built the pillars of sanctity."

The idea of a civilization based on the spirituality of work still awaits an adequate elaboration, both theoretically and practically, requiring an immense ecumenical synthesis of Jewish, Catholic, Protestant, Muslim and other traditions.

Among the U.S. sources for a spirituality of work is Father Isaac Hecker, founder of the Paulists. Hecker, ahead of his time, saw the possibility of integration between work and religion. He grasped the insight that every culture develops its own worldview and ethos. To be successful, Hecker knew, evangelization has to build on the unique cultural characteristics of a people. The U.S. culture, as he saw it, was activist; directing its energies toward the mastery of nature and the environment. It was in that context that he predicted in 1863 that the ethos of the American future was to be a spirituality of work: "Our age is not an age of martyrdom, nor an age of hermits, nor a monastic age. Although it has its martyrs, its recluses and its monastic communities, these are not and are not likely to be its prevailing types of Christian perfection. Our age lives in its busy marts, in counting-rooms, in workshops, in homes and in the varied relations that form human society, and it is into these that sanctity is to be introduced.… Out of the cares, toils, duties, afflictions and responsibilities of daily life are to be built the pillars of sanctity."

One of the major roadblocks to a revitalization of our way of thinking about work is language itself. After all, worldviews and models of reality are embedded in language, and the language and images we use to describe work often fail to keep pace with the changing reality of work and thus fail to reflect *the new meanings of work* that are emerging. Daniel Bell in *The Coming of Post-Industrial Society* argues that the image of the mass production line, which once captured accurately the rhythm of work, is out of date. Bell finds no adequate images of work today.

Nevertheless, the minute division of labor that first appeared in factory production has now invaded all areas of labor: the office, the research lab, the hospital and the university. Few persons today work in isolation. Their productive effort is usually only one small part of a much larger process. Yet while modern work has become socialized to an amazing degree, the highly individualistic thought patterns of our culture prevent the new meaning of work from being integrated into a positive work ethos.

John Dewey in *Individualism Old and New* noted this discrepancy: "Our material culture, as anthropologists would call it, is verging upon the collective and the corporate. Our moral culture, along with our ideology is, on the other hand, still saturated with ideals and values from an individualism derived from the pre-scientific, pre-technical age."

The secular language of *service* that all occupations and professions cling to in legitimizing their work to the public has been worn thin and eroded by a deep-seated skepticism regarding the motives of economic agents. It can be argued that a return to religious sources can retrieve the notion of service, but religious language itself needs to invent ways of legitimizing mixed motives—showing how one can work for self and at the same time work for the community. The very language of spirituality seems more appropriate in a Benedictine monastery than in a modern office. Yet the notion of spirituality is by no means exclusively a religious concept. The secularized understanding of spirituality is even more widespread than its religious one. Dewey used *spirituality* to mean the humanistic values of a people and their culture and thus it is a norm against which to measure the fruits of an economic system. How to integrate the secular and the religious meanings of spirituality into a work ethic remains a difficult and challenging question for both religion and the U.S. culture.

As a modest beginning I suggest a hermeneutics of the cultural expressions now referring to work. Such an exercise may uncover the various ways the self and work are modeled in our culture.

We have a wide variety of different words to identify our work: *career, vocation, profession.* We often use the terms interchangeably; and in one sense, it does not make much difference if we do. But sometimes what appears to be merely a semantic preference in fact conceals a perception of reality. For example, in parliamentary forms of government, it is common to use the word *minister* as a title—like Prime Minister. The word *minister*, of course, is an ancient Christian term referring to service. When *minister* was first applied to governmental work something of the original meaning of *service* must have been implied, thus reflecting how people at that time thought about work—in this case, public work.

In the same way, behind our current vocabulary for discussing work there lurk different models of thinking about the self and work. For example, what worldview does the concept of *career* contain? It seems to point exclusively to the self and individual fulfillment, rather than also pointing outward to the community and the common good. In the long run, when career becomes careerism, it may prove fatal even to the self. In a fascinating study of the corporate executive, Michael Maccoby in *The Gamesman* says that careerism results not only in constant anxiety, but more importantly, in an underdeveloped heart. Maccoby describes high school students who have become involved in the community because they thought colleges would favor the involved student. "These students had become careerists, their decisions were determined not out of a sense of vocation, but in terms of career."

What if, instead of using career as an organizing model of work, we used *vocation*? A vocation demands that we search our unique gifts, it demands self-knowledge and, at the same time, calls for an effort to convert our gifts into a service for others, for the community. There is an intimacy in the way the concept of *vocation* links us to work. When we say that teaching is a vocation, we convey a sense of personal dedication that is absent if we use, instead, *career*. Those without a vocation find life empty. To be without a vocation, says Ed Marciniak, is the worst kind of unemployment.

Catholics, of course, have a lot of catching up to do since they have traditionally restricted the meaning of vocation to the priesthood or religious life. Vatican II took a gigantic step forward in its efforts to re-appropriate the notion of vocation by applying it equally to secular pursuits. Vatican II's *Pastoral Constitution on the Church in the Modern World* refers continually to the human person's total vocation, thus moving toward an integration of religion and secular tasks. If vocation implies that our work is essentially a service we perform for one another, then churches will have to be reminded that the secular division of labor, our work, is the original and primordial form of ministry.

If a careerist approach to life and occupation inclines one to buckle under the pressure of the status quo, then a vocational approach seems to imply a shaping of one's own deeds and altering the world a little through one's vocation. Such an understanding of vocation appreciates the potential for social justice and for social change that lies at the dynamic core of the ordinary roles of factory worker, businessman and businesswomen, mayor, lawyer, nurse; thus balancing the view that

> GOOD WORK ENABLES each of us, in cooperation with others, to be of service and to liberate ourselves from inborn egocentricity.

institutions can only be changed from the outside. The concerns for justice and peace can be translated into the moral strategy of each occupation and profession, for it is in work and the division of labor that the secrets of a culture lie hidden.

The notion of work as a vocation developed in a society of limited occupational opportunities, of crafts and trades requiring such long periods of apprenticeship that for all practical purposes the choice of an occupation was a choice for life. How viable is vocation as a model in a society characterized by specialization, and where a person may have five or seven different occupations in a lifetime?

For this and other reasons, we may prefer the notion of *good work* as our model, rather than vocation. Good work, says E.F. Schumacher, provides necessary goods and services. It enables everyone to use, and thereby perfect, other gifts like good stewards. Good work enables each of us, in cooperation with others, to be of service and to liberate ourselves from our inborn egocentricity.

The notion of good work includes the best features of the other models, especially of vocation. It has the advantage of equalizing all work, discouraging invidious comparisons between manual and intellectual work, between so-called professional and non-professional work. The corporate executive and the janitor, the computer programmer and the sanitary worker have this in common: each is called to do good work. The notion of good work is attractive because it calls forth a respect for the job to be done, a feeling of faithfulness and responsibility. It balances a concern for the good of the worker with a healthy concern for the good of the work. It also supplies a set of criteria by which to measure the *goodness* of our structure of occupations. It thus can serve as a guide to society that desires to renew its work life, both ethically and socially.

The search for a new model of self and work is necessary because the meaning of work has undergone a profound transformation, so profound that our language and spiritualities have not yet caught up with it. For the first time in modern history a civilization based on work, accepted and acknowledged as such, has become a viable idea. To discern the new meanings of work will require overcoming the barriers of traditional language and concepts.

John Paul II's *On Human Work* is remarkable for catching a glimpse of the new meaning of work. It is an attempt to find a language that reflects the reality. To suggest, as he does, that the bread produced by the work of our hands is not only the bread that keeps us alive, but also "the bread of science and progress, civilization and culture" is already a reversal of traditional thought patterns and a new way of imagining work.

LET THE LAITY BE LAITY
by Russell Barta

A new phrase, *lay ministry*, has apparently found a permanent home in the vocabulary of Catholics. We hear the phrase bandied about on college campuses, in graduate programs in theology, in diocesan offices and in the local parish. "You are called to lay ministry," Catholics are being told.

An extraordinary number of lay people are responding to the call and are now in the sanctuary performing various tasks once the sole province of the priest. They are also accepting responsibilities for other Church-related activities: youth ministers, religious education ministers, extraordinary ministers and the like. Just as a doctor surrounds himself or herself with a supporting group of nurses and other technical assistants, so too the priest extends his work by calling on a supporting team of lay ministers.

It is precisely this almost exclusive preoccupation with involving lay people in Church-related tasks that has some of us—priests and laity—worried.

During Advent 1977 a group of us issued the *Chicago Declaration of Christian Concern* [reprinted in this book] in which we lamented the fact that a truncated, narrow vision of the laity's role was replacing the broad vision developed by Vatican II. What concerns us is that lay ministry as now understood has crowded out and completely overshadowed that other dimension of lay life—the dimension which Vatican II regarded as unique: The laity serving the kingdom of God in the marketplace of business, commerce, the trades, the arts, the various professions and in politics. The *Chicago Declaration of Christian Concern* argues that the laity's work-in-the-world is being devalued.

No one can read Vatican II and the social encyclicals without feeling the passion of those documents to direct the spiritual resources of the church toward the transformation of the world. And the strategic role in that transformation is realistically assigned to the laity, for it is they who typically have access to the world through their occupational and professional involvements. They are the church-in-the-world as bricklayers, bus drivers, lawyers, politicians and white-collar workers—not as extraordinary ministers or lectors at Mass.

Unless the laity see the competence and moral vision which they bring to their everyday work as their unique road to sanctity, the church is only spinning its wheels when it talks about the Christian vocation to bring justice and charity to world affairs....

> ## WHY DO SO MANY
> pastors address their parishioners
> as if the 40 or more hours of work
> during the previous week
> is irrelevant to what is going on
> in church?

When was the last time any of us heard a homily on the meaning of work? Why do so many pastors address their parishioners as if the 40 or more hours of work during the previous week is irrelevant to what is going on in church? How many retreats given in the past year centered on the need for renewal within the various occupations and professions? How many Catholic colleges today require their graduates to have studied the social teachings of the church? Why isn't a fully developed theology of work one of the top priorities of our theologians?

Such serious neglect of Catholics as church-in-the-world ironically comes at a time when U.S. society is undergoing the pains of its own renewal. Every profession and institution today is subject to serious moral scrutiny. Law, medicine, education, business, engineering and government are being forced to look at themselves in the mirror of ethical reflection. It would be a terrible irony if the church, preoccupied with its own renewal, closed its eyes to the creative role it could play in the renewal of society through people alert to their Christian responsibilities.

Catholicism has always had a difficult time coming to grips with the religious significance of lay life. For centuries, it was ambivalent about marriage and marital sex. Lay life was frequently regarded as spiritually second best. And even efforts in the past to help the laity think religiously about their lives usually resulted in a watered-down version of some monastic ideal, *a spirituality for the laity rather than a lay spirituality*.

Vatican II made a valiant effort to capture the religious meaning of Catholics immersion into worldly tasks; but its central insights have been buried under an avalanche of ministry rhetoric that turns the attention of Catholics inward rather than outward....

Since World War II, Catholics have made dramatic inroads into the middle class and now as never before honeycomb important economic, political and professional establishments. Unfortunately, in our upward mobility, Catholics have not had the support of a dynamic theology of work and professional life. This theology would assist us in constructing a religious interpretation of our new economic and professional responsibilities and protect us from secular *careerism* which is now so rampant....

It would be ironic and tragic if, at this opportune moment, middle class Catholics were lost to the church.

MONSIGNOR JOHN EGAN

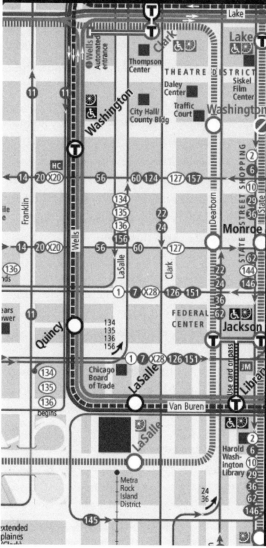

1916 - 2001

One day in the fall of 1997 I met Monsignor John (Jack) Egan for lunch at the Cliff Dwellers Club. My agenda was some crucial issue, which I can no longer recall. By that time, I had known Egan fairly well for at least sixteen years and been acquainted with him for over twenty-five. But he began lunch with the deceptively simple question: "What's your story?" For the next hour Egan elicited most of the current twists and turns of my life. It was as if we had no urgent business to conduct, as if no issues of mutual interest were pressing on our city or church. He was a pastor to me during that lunch, and I know for a fact that hundreds of other Chicagoans—Catholic and non-Catholic alike—had similar experiences with this feisty Irish-American priest. Egan built his Rolodex retail, listening to people one-by-one and often sending a hand-written note to follow up on a meeting.

> IT'S NOT THAT EGAN
> woke up each day spoiling for a
> fight. But he was determined to get
> people thinking.

Out of Egan's lifelong habit of listening to people came scores of organizations and campaigns. Ordained in 1943 and assigned as associate pastor to Saint Justin Martyr parish on Chicago's south side, he became a chaplain to the Young Christian Students and the Young Christian Workers as well as director of the Cana Conference from 1947 to 1958. In those positions, he bonded with hundreds of individuals and couples, forging lifelong relationships. He developed marriage preparation programs and materials that, with revisions, are still in use today.

During the 1960s, Egan was director of the Office of Urban Affairs for the Archdiocese of Chicago. There he collaborated with Saul Alinsky and Edward Chambers on several community organization efforts, eventually becoming a key member of the Industrial Areas Foundation board of directors.

On the outs with Cardinal John Cody of Chicago (for reasons obvious to anyone who was in Chicago at the time), Egan spent the 1970s and early 1980s at the University of Notre Dame at the invitation of Father Theodore Hesburgh, CSC, where he headed the Institute for Pastoral and Social Ministry and, with his assistant Peggy Roach, facilitated the activities of the Catholic Committee for Urban Ministry.

Egan returned to Chicago in 1983 to direct the Office of Human Relations and Ecumenism for the Archdiocese, and upon his "retirement" he became the director of the Office of Community Affairs at DePaul University, which is where he was when he died in 2001. (A statue of Egan by Chicago sculptress Margot McMahon, daughter of artist Franklin McMahon, now stands outside the Student Union at DePaul's Lincoln Park campus, asking students, "What have you done for justice?")

Egan was perhaps the best-known disciple of Monsignor Reynold Hillenbrand, the pioneering rector of Chicago's major seminary in the late 1930s.

Hillenbrand was the founding father for the confident Chicago-style of Catholic thought and action that Egan and his friends came to embody.

In one of our conversations, Egan predicted that Hillenbrand would be forgotten once Egan's own generation of priests and lay leaders died. "Reynie didn't write any books," Egan bemoaned.

Egan wanted to know if, for similar reasons, he too might be forgotten over the years. Except for one out-of-print book on housing he coauthored, all of Egan's writing was in short articles and outlines for hundreds of talks. He was a master of the short, pointed note typed on a half-sheet of stationary or on a postcard, not the book-length manuscript.

I would receive one of those notes from Egan several times a year, commenting on something I wrote or on some topic of mutual interest. His reaction to some of my articles, to tell the truth, was sharply critical. The criticisms were often along the lines of: "Enough pontificating; do more organizing."

It's not that Egan woke up each day spoiling for a fight. But he was determined to get people thinking. An incident from a stroll I had with him in the Loop (Chicago's downtown) was typical. Early one evening Egan and I were on our way, probably to a tavern, when not surprisingly we passed a paraplegic panhandler. "I don't like it when beggars put their disability on display," this champion of the poor said to me. So, OK, how was I to reply? Either way, Egan had a lesson to impart. If I said, "I don't like it either," Egan would reply, "But you've never been forced to beg." If I said, "He has a right to beg," Egan would reply, "You should change the economic system so he doesn't have to." (I gave the guy a couple of bucks, which shut the Monsignor up.)

On the day of his ordination, in addition to his public vows, Egan made a private vow "to work for the enhancement of the lay role in the church." In subsequent years, Egan and the leaders he nurtured made major contributions to ecumenism (especially in Jewish/Catholic dialogue), to marriage preparation, to family life ministry, to labor relations, to the community organization movement and more.

With Greg Pierce, I visited Egan just three days before he died. He urged us to interest more young lay leaders in the connections to be discovered between work, faith, social justice and liturgy. Egan reminded us that no Christian could be entirely comfortable until every single person has meaningful work in an environment that affords a living wage.

"We must develop a pastoral strategy that affirms and supports the work of our people in their jobs, their communities, in our culture and society," Egan told the priests of Portland, Oregon, in April 1986. "It is not a question of priests becoming prophets or politicians. It is to recognize that we and our people share a similar problem: how to insure our integrity in the midst of the messy business of daily life."

In a 1979 talk in Fort Lauderdale, he said: "What we need today in the church is not talent or energy or commitment; all of these we have in abundance. What we need is a sense of purpose, a renewal of mission, a challenging program of action—we need to get to work. We need Catholic doctors who will take the lead in reshaping our medical system to ensure that the health needs of our people are met. We need Catholic lawyers and judges and police and corrections officers to reform our criminal justice system. We need men and women of Catholic wisdom, committed to justice and peace, sitting in corporations and trade unions and community organizations and government agencies. We need scholars unafraid to deal with science and society, with the humanities and the arts with reference to basic values and transcendent human possibilities."

On the occasion of the 50th anniversary of his ordination, Egan invited 800 of his "close friends" to a party at a plumbers' union hall on Chicago's near west side. There he distributed a holy card with this quotation from Cardinal Emmanuel Suhard of Paris (1874-1949): "One cannot be a saint and live the gospel we preach without spending oneself to provide everyone with housing, employment, food, leisure and education—without which life is no longer meaningful."

Egan's papers are archived at the University of Notre Dame. His biography, *An Alley in Chicago: the Ministry of a City Priest* by Margery Frisbie (Sheed & Ward, 1991), is still available. The book's title is taken from a well-traveled and well-connected monsignor who many years ago, at a dinner Egan attended, said: "I have seen the great boulevards of the world. The boulevards of Rome. The boulevards of Paris. The boulevards of Rio de Janeiro. They are all grand. But I would rather have an alley in Chicago than any one of them." So too, Frisbie writes, Egan's spirits always "lifted at the thought of the vital, demanding, electrifying energy symbolized by Chicago's alleys."

LITURGY AND JUSTICE:
AN UNFINISHED AGENDA

by Monsignor John J. Egan

There is a certain irony in reflecting on the relationship between liturgy and social justice.

On the one hand, as the churches of Central and South America have taught us, and as Christian feminists are emphasizing, the relationship between liturgical celebration and the practice of justice is probably the most significant and certainly one of the most urgent questions calling for liturgists' attention today. If there is any dimension of the liturgy which promises to alter our practice and transform our identity as a celebrating people, it is this connection to justice.

And yet—and this is where the irony is so striking—the connection was entirely missed at the Second Vatican Council.

The importance of liturgical reform for the renewal of church life is openly acknowledged in the opening paragraph of Vatican II's *Constitution on the Sacred Liturgy*, and yet the document never returns in any explicit way to the problem of the connection between liturgy and the social life of the faithful, or the role of the church in the world.

The same break is only confirmed by the otherwise splendid achievement of Vatican II's *Pastoral Constitution on the Church in the Modern World*. Its broad vision of the heights and depths of the human condition and of the role of the church in forwarding the redemptive work of God for the benefit of all humanity utterly omits any mention of the place of the liturgy as source and summit of this process.

In this way, Vatican II, by its silence, lends sad confirmation to what was a fact of life in the 1960s: the failure of Christian people and Christian leaders to acknowledge the essential connection between liturgy and society, much less liturgy and social justice.

This is one [underappreciated] reason for all the confusion that arose following the Second Vatican Council. Initially, liturgical reform was expected to revitalize the communal life of the church. If liturgy was the public, communal

worship of the church, then it seemed that a liturgy marked by vernacular language, greater congregational participation, and adaptation to the needs and
concerns of particular groups would bring about an intensification of community, a deeper faith and a more active sense of mission.

DO YOU REFORM
the liturgy to create community,
or, renew community to create
good liturgy?

When this proved not to be the
case, when liturgical reform became
as often a source of division as of
renewed community, commenta-
tors began to say that we had first to
renew community life and only then
would a new sense of community
find expression in the liturgy. This chicken and egg argument—do you reform
the liturgy to create community, or, renew community to create good liturgy?—
continues to plague us, reflecting our failure to probe the depths of the relationship which must exist between faith and life, worship and work, liturgy and social
responsibility.

The fact of the matter was that in most countries, then as now, the people
involved in the liturgical movement rarely if ever had any contact with those
engaged in the social apostolate. These two great developments in 20th-century
Catholic life moved ahead on parallel lines and have yet to make real contact.

To say that they *never* met is an exaggeration, for there were a few people—
very few—who moved in both circles and managed to combine in their lives and
works the values of liturgical renewal with a profound concern for social justice.
Chief among them, mainly because he was the only one of them who waged his
apostolate through the printed word, was Father Virgil Michel, OSB of Minnesota.
His writings served as a source of inspiration and encouragement to those in the
1930s and 1940s who labored in the cities and in rural communities to uphold the
dignity of the laborer and the rights of the worker and who also saw in the liturgy
the source and paradigm of the church's concern for justice.

Unfortunately, such people as Father Michel were too few and made little
impact beyond their own immediate pastoral sphere or in a few Catholic Worker
communities. In Europe, where the main impetus for liturgical reform was developing, they were even fewer....

Cooperation between the liturgy apostolate and the social apostolate weakened after Father Michel's death in 1938, so that by the late 1950s, even in this country, it had virtually disappeared. Its voice was not heard in the planning for reform that went on *before* Vatican II; liturgy and justice went their own ways *during* and *after* the Council.

Now the opportunity arises again, thanks partly to the influence of the church's rapidly developing social teaching and to the questions it is forcing us to confront…

For this reason, it might be well for us to return to the heritage that Father Virgil Michel left us—a heritage kept alive by such outstanding pastoral priests as Monsignor Reynold Hillenbrand, Father H.A. Reinhold and Monsignor Dan Cantwell. It is a heritage developed in this country and in response to the socio-economic situation of this country.…

Today's justice issues are very different and the wealth of theoretical resources is vaster, but there were certain basic principles which we would do well to recover. [In particular,] Father Virgil Michel [believed] that the prime resource of the church in its effort to redeem humankind from the perniciousness of anti-humanistic philosophies is its awareness of itself as the body of Christ…

In the Catholic Worker houses where the liturgical movement enjoyed its first and most consistent audience, the doctrine of the Mystical Body, central to the spirituality of Dorothy Day, drew forth a profound consciousness of solidarity with the church, and through the church with all other persons, most especially the poor. It was this consciousness of being members one with another in Christ that distinguished the social apostolate of the Catholic Worker from others, elevating both the middle-class youth who adopted voluntary poverty and the poor guests who came to the Houses of Hospitality to a new and empowering union of one with the other in Christ's mystical body.

Over against the subordination of the person to the state, or the canonization of self-interest in a capitalistic society, Father Michel and Dorothy Day saw in the organic model of the body of Christ a profound affirmation of the fact that the welfare of the society and the dignity of the individual are inseparable: for the individual only achieves personal fulfillment within the vital network of a supportive and respectful society of persons, while the society as a whole is only as healthy as its respect for even the least human person. By drawing attention to the outcasts, the "least among us" the Catholic Workers challenged both church and society to a new vision of human solidarity.

THE RECOVERY OF THE SENSE of the church as community is one of the undeniable gains of the liturgical reforms of Vatican II.

The doctrine of the Mystical Body thus constituted a profoundly theological *a priori* both for the liturgical movement and the social apostolate. The necessity for both the renewal of worship and the reconstruction of the social order were, for Father Michel rooted in the Incarnation—an Incarnation seen as essentially in continuity with the created order and not in contradiction of it.

In accordance with Catholic belief, Father Michel saw the natural law governing human life in its personal and social dimensions to be affirmed and elevated, not destroyed, by the redemptive work of God in Jesus Christ: there could be no distinction between theology and anthropology, no separation of the orders of nature and grace, no contradiction between the nature of the church as expressed in the liturgy and the ideal of human life as criterion of every social order, from the level of the family to that of international relations…

Conversely, he identified the problems of contemporary Christianity as identical at root with the problems of contemporary society. Both were the result of a profound individualism which had permeated both the Western world and the Western church. The ultimate cure for the evils of both was for Christians to become aware of their true identity, to remember the dignity that was theirs, and to accept their mission as baptized persons to continue the redemptive and reconciling work of Christ in a world divided and sacrificed to the pursuit of unbridled self-interest or to the omnipotence of the state.

Of course, the recovery of the sense of the church as community is one of the undeniable gains of the liturgical reforms of Vatican II. This is certainly so, yet one is forced to wonder, at this point in history, whether we have really grasped the meaning of the communitarian character of the church.

While strengthening our congregational sense, have we lost our awareness of that larger body of Christ of which each community is both an expression and a part? The introduction of the vernacular, of new music, of lay ministries, of celebration facing the people, have transformed our style of celebration, but it remains to be proved that we have transformed our awareness or our sense of solidarity with one another, let alone our sense of solidarity with those who are not of our class, or nation, or color.

There is even evidence to suggest that the emphasis on celebrating as a community has led Catholics to desert the mixed congregations that once characterized Catholic worship, as opposed to Protestant worship. Instead, some Catholics today search on Sunday for groups of like-minded people, or at least for more satisfying kinds of liturgy. In other words, it may be that the emphasis on community participation since Vatican II has contributed to a worsening of the problem of Christian individualism, by identifying the required sense of community with various comfortable ways of being together with your own kind…

At the present time, there can be no doubt that the whole concept of the worshiping community needs to be re-thought. We have taken the agenda of Vatican II as a call to holding hands in the liturgy and sharing coffee with our own kind afterwards. The image of the Mystical Body, however, suggests that Christian community is not something which needs to be invented so much as it needs to be discovered.

In other words, we perhaps need to recognize Vatican II's call for communitarian liturgy less as an invitation to adopt various community-building techniques than as being, first and foremost, a call to recognize the common life that is ours in the Spirit and, beyond that, the common humanity we share with every other human being on the face of God's earth.

Without this primary reflection, and the conversion of mind and heart it calls for, our liturgies are likely to continue to be more or less cozy affirmations of who we like to think we are, and the cause of justice will continue to be neglected…

At a time when our documents of social justice are stronger than ever, we need to be reminded that words and committees do not change the world. "Neither paper programs nor high-sounding, unfulfilled resolutions once renewed the world," Father Michel wrote, "but new and living persons born out of the depths of Christianity."

Liturgical reform, without that conversion, remains what social activists have often accused it of being: a form of self-indulgence for those with the luxury of being able to indulge in such things.

> # THE LITURGICAL ASSEMBLY
> needs to become truly catholic, not only in its composition but, more importantly, in its intention.

The liturgical assembly, then, needs to become truly catholic, not only in its composition but, more importantly, in its intention. Only in that way can the liturgy be the source and paradigm of the just society.

Conversely, social activists who see in the liturgy only a source of personal strength, unrelated to their striving for justice, or who abandon the liturgy of the church altogether as an irrelevance, effectively disassociate their social and political activities from the larger plan and purpose of God which the liturgy is intended to recall and to realize....

It would be interesting to speculate whether the abandonment of the Mystical Body metaphor after Vatican II, in favor of the image of the people of God, which is more flexible and less organic, might have contributed to the loss of social and ecclesial consciousness at a time when we thought we were recovering it. Whatever of that, it remains the case that the emphasis of Father Michel and the early liturgical-social apostolate on the importance of the image of the body of Christ might be worth reconsidering, even if both ecclesial and social conditions have moved far beyond what they were all those years ago.

IN PRAISE OF VATICAN II
by Monsignor John J. Egan

I was fortunate to have lived before, during and after Pope John XXIII's pontificate. Sadly, many who had that same advantage only seem to remember the church before him as the "Glorious 1950s." Many say that he was a sweet old man who brought unintended changes to our church from which we shall probably never recover.

They really know very little of the church in the time before Vatican II and the tremendous steps which were taken by all of the bishops during that wonderful period of the early 1960s. It was Vatican II that brought so many needed changes in our worship and in the activities of the church—the role of the laity, our relationship to other religions, to the world in general, to the priests, the bishops, and the place of the pope himself in the governance of the church of Christ.

Toward the end of the Vatican II, our own Monsignor George Higgins hosted a dinner in one of the hotels overlooking the Vatican.

Father John Courtney Murray, SJ addressing the priests that night said: "Gentlemen, we shall see coming from this Vatican Council some 30 years of confusion, but after that we shall see a glorious church emerge."

Was he correct? We have certainly seen the confusion, but Murray could not have foreseen the [problems] which we witnessed from the middle 1960s to the present time.

So what does this do to the legacy of Blessed Pope John XXIII and of Vatican II?

I remember Father Tom McDonough saying to me on the plane coming back from Rome after the Council: "Jack, get worried. The Curia will now take over and ignore what was done in Vatican II and refer to it as *that occurrence back in the 1960s* and go on ruling the Church in the way they have always done."

I have tried, ever so falteringly, to live my life in the years since Vatican II according to the maxims and the teaching of John XXIII, while recognizing the extraordinary life and work of our present Holy Father. As an outside observer to Vatican II, it was the Curia that bothered me—not only during the Council sessions, but still today.

Let me say, as Father Richard McBrien states in his wonderful *Lives of the Popes* that John XXIII made it clear in his opening address to the Council that it had not been called, as previous Councils had been, to refute errors and to clarify points of doctrine.

> AS AN OUTSIDE OBSERVER
> to Vatican II, it was the Curia that bothered me.

"The substance of the ancient doctrine of the deposit of faith is one thing," John XXIII said, "and the way in which it is presented is another. And it is the latter that must be taken into great consideration, with patience if necessary, everything being measured in the form and proportion of a magisterium which is predominantly pastoral in character."

He acknowledged that the Church had punished those in error in the past with much severity, but he insisted that nowadays, "the Spouse of Christ prefers to make use of the medicine of mercy rather than that of severity. She considers that she meets the needs of the present day by demonstrating the validity of her teaching rather than by condemnations."

The most effective means of eradicating discord and of promoting harmony, peace and unity, John XXIII wrote, is through the spreading everywhere of "the fullness of Christian charity."

That opening address, one of the most important pronouncements in his entire pontificate, placed John XXIII in direct opposition to leading figures in the Roman Curia who held to a more authoritarian, defensive and punitive vision of the church.

"In the daily exercise of our office," he pointed out, "we sometimes have to listen, much to our regret, to voices of persons who, though burning with zeal, are not endowed with too much sense of discretion. In these modern times they can see nothing but prevarication and ruin. They say that our era, in comparison with the past eras, is getting worse, and they have learned nothing from history, which is nonetheless, the teacher of life. We disagree with these prophets of doom.... In the present order of things, Divine Providence is leading us to a new order of human relations. And everything, even human differences, leads us to the greater good of the church."

This I always believed, and I have tried to live my life by this vision. The Vatican II document, Gaudium et Spes states boldly: "The joys and the hopes, the grief and the anxieties of the men and women of this age" are primary concerns of the church. This document provides a new vision of the relation between the church and the world, claiming that the church and the world learn from each other.

These are just a few of the things which I learned from Vatican II and therefore from John XXIII. They have fashioned my life and my ministry in labor relations, in social action in general, and in the human problems facing all of our people.

I shall always be grateful for Vatican II.

FATHER DENNIS GEANEY, OSA

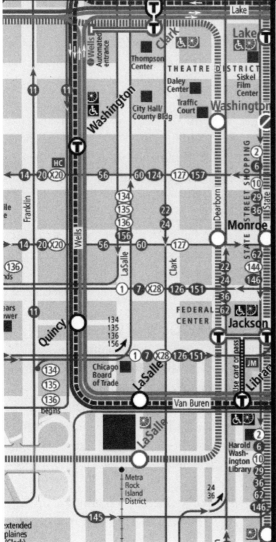

1914 - 1992

I first met Father Dennis Geaney, OSA, in the early 1980s when I was running a support group for the unemployed. For the next dozen years we talked weekly, either by phone or in person, as he would often spend his day off at my parish, Saint Clare of Montefalco on the Southwest Side. I edited some of Geaney's manuscripts, including his final book, *The Quest for Community*. He was a guest at our home for dinner many times during his final months, until he died in 1992.

Every conversation with Geaney included his reaction to a recent book or article. Something in *America*, *Commonweal* or another magazine always seemed to "completely change my thinking" or was "a real shocker."

That was a refreshing dimension to Geaney: Even in his seventies, all things were new and exciting to him.

Geaney was a good example of the power of the storyteller. He had chronic heart problems and tried to walk every day. His regular bulletin column, "Confessions of a Streetwalker," chronicled what he discovered on those walks.

A typical column starts innocuously. "Don't be alarmed," Geaney writes, "if I take a flask out of my pocket in a restaurant that does not have a liquor license. The flask contains low sodium, low calorie, red wine vinegar salad dressing. I'm not about to ask the waitress the sodium level of each salad dressing." Geaney invariably goes on to deliver a lesson. "I had a fine dinner for $5.95," he continues. "I asked the waitress how the restaurant can make a profit. 'Cheap labor,' she replied. Two other waitresses filled in the facts. Their base pay is $2.10 plus tips. The IRS gets its share of the presumed 15% tip. If a cheapo tips less than 15%, the waitress still pays taxes on what the tightwad did not give. If waitresses ever picket, don't be shocked to see me carrying a sign."

> SOCIAL JUSTICE IS BEST
> crafted by thoughtful Christians in
> and through their daily work

Geaney was born in South Boston, where his father was a peddler, and educated in Washington, DC. He then spent the next fifty-four years in the Chicago area. An order priest, he was introduced to Monsignor Reynold Hillenbrand and the Chicago-style of church by Monsignor Bill Quinn, a leader in ministry to migrants. Geaney was attracted to Chicago because, in his opinion, it was "the Catholic Action capital of the world for an admittedly small movement of priests, seminarians and young lay people who were thrilled by the raw gospel message." Geaney became a chaplain to many Catholic Action groups, including the Young Christian Workers, the Young Christian Students and the Christian Family Movement. Later in his career he was the first director of field education at the Catholic Theological Union in Hyde Park and an associate pastor at St. Victor's parish in Calumet City, Illinois.

Unlike Hillenbrand and many of his disciples, Geaney was always at the keyboard, typing his thoughts. He wrote several books about the Vatican II changes in the church. Some of his writing on that topic actually anticipated Vatican II. In addition to his weekly bulletin column, Geaney also edited a monthly newsletter for Chicago priests titled simply *Upturn*. (The Chicago caucus in heaven reportedly publishes an ongoing commentary on mortal life. It is appropriately titled *Downturn*.)

Geaney's literary output was amazing, especially considering that he didn't publish his first article until he was in his late thirties. In fact, he told me that first article "received more attention and requests for reprints than any other piece I ever wrote." In that 1951 article for *Orate Fratres*, Geaney "challenged liturgists to connect liturgy with daily life." As he often explained to me, liturgy and workaday life are nearly the same. The Greek word *leitourgia*, from which comes the English word *liturgy*, means roughly "the work of the people performed in the public square." Thus Geaney bemoaned the false division within the ranks of church leaders between the "social justice types" and the "liturgy types." Proclaiming the gospel requires the perfection of liturgical ceremonies, Geaney said, but making it "too much a sacristy affair" dangerously removes liturgy and preaching "from the monotony of the assembly line, the smoke-filled room of politics, and the difficulty of family life."

Likewise, social justice is best crafted by thoughtful Christians in and through their daily work, Geaney believed. "The laity must not become clerical assistants, but must assume their rightful place as confirmed Christians in solving the specific problems for which they are solely responsible."

Of all the Vatican II changes, Geaney thought the removal of the altar rail was the most significant, because it put the Eucharist and daily work in closer proximity. "Although it is difficult to appreciate sometimes," he wrote, "the work of growers, truck drivers, grocers, accountants and service people really becomes the stuff of the bread and wine, the body and blood of Christ that we take into our hands to eat and drink. The sacraments we celebrate in a church building are simply lifting up what happens on the streets. The divine food and drink of the sacraments in turn is carried into our daily work. When God is really experienced in the liturgy, She will be found in homes, offices and factories."

HILLENBRAND AND THE SHIFT TO VATICAN II
by Father Dennis Geaney, OSA

From the 1940s to the 1960s, the priests in Chicago were number one in the country in pioneering Catholic Action (lay formation), social action and the liturgical movement. It stemmed from one man, the charismatic rector of St. Mary of the Lake Seminary from 1936-1944, Monsignor Reynold Hillenbrand. His disciples, now retired or deceased, set fires in neighborhoods as they hit the pavement on their first assignments after ordination. In the late 1960s, the movement began to sputter and die. Church historians of the next century will critique this movement that has left its mark on the North American church, but I can't wait. I have a compulsion to pull it together for myself.

Reiny Hillenbrand on a Meyers-Briggs Test, which he would disdain, would come out an I and T (Introvert and Thinker). Before these psychological categories, he would be identified as saint, seer and poet. In touch with the pre-Vatican II theological stirrings in the Louvain and with the fresh approach to young workers pioneered by Cardinal Joseph Cardijn of Brussels, Reiny was able to translate European breakthroughs into North American lay movements. The papal social encyclicals became a filter for his interpretation of the gospels and his platform for taking on the economic and political establishments. He translated the liturgical revival coming out of the monasteries of Europe and Collegeville, Minnesota into parish liturgical renewal. In his big speeches at national liturgical weeks, at the seminary or wherever two or three hundred priests were gathered in the name of the Lord, Reiny would paint the big picture with repetitive phrases and dramatic cadences and liturgical gestures that translated the theology of the Mystical Body into action programs that responded to the concerns of work, neighborhood, family and parish.

How do I explain the waning of Reiny's charisma more than a decade before he died in 1979? Indeed, ill health plagued him for years, but I perceived it as his inability to shift to the new theology so influential in Vatican II documents. He never saw human freedom as central to the Christian life. His 19th and early 20th century papal blueprints for reordering society and the church became dysfunctional as we entered the era of Vatican II, which sponsored a pilgrim church, people going with the flow, trusting the Spirit to pull together our brokenness. Vatican II theology pulled the rug from under Reiny's hierarchical theology of the laity, social action and liturgy. The ecclesiastical structures out of which his avant-garde disciplines were working were falling apart and the disintegration is not yet finished.

> OUR PERSONAL CREDIBILITY
> as priests hangs on how we do justice
> to our lay people.

Reiny's genius lay in his insight that lay formation, social action and liturgy were integrative elements of a new church, but the intuition could not flower under his authoritarian thumb in a North American church that had a new awareness of a democratic spirit. Reiny's trilogy would have to wait for a church from below to evolve new structures.

Our personal credibility as priests hangs on how we do justice to our lay people. The Catholic Action notion of the priest as the animator [or hands on coach] of lay people is dead. It is the lay people themselves who will take the reins of leadership in public life, without our explicit direction. The psychological thrust of pastoral theology after Vatican II indeed turned us inward, but it was not regression. We need a period of maturation before we find our bearings in this sea of change. Lay formation, social action and liturgy will take new shapes as they emerge from the new mold.

WORK: A LOST IDENTITY
by Father Dennis J. Geaney, OSA

I t was a colorful procession making its way up the aisle of Chicago's Holy Name Cathedral, but it was not like the pageantry of the burial of a cardinal or the installation of his successor. It was a people's procession. The focus was not on the pomp and status of the presiding prelates but—as it was in the early church—on the people who made up the assembly. What caught everyone's eye as they turned to watch the procession was not a bishop's miter but a colorful standard held high by a layperson flanked by other lay people. Each standard, held high above the congregation bore the emblem and the name of a Chicago union local: Pipe Fitters, Local 597; Machine Workers of America, District II; International Brotherhood of Electrical Workers, Local 1859; Office and Professional Employees, Local 28.

The Chicago Labor Day Mass in the 1950s was not sponsored by Holy Name Cathedral but by the Catholic Labor Alliance of Chicago, which also produced a lively newspaper appropriately named *Work*. It was the Chicago Catholic working force's finest hour. For one brief moment in history the center of a cathedral liturgy was the working people celebrating their giftedness as artisans and laborers, as extensions of God's creation—a giftedness for which they could give praise and thanks. For this brief period a group of lay Catholics ritualized in an urban setting what Catholics had done for centuries in an agricultural society.

Why did this holy alliance of work and worship, which lasted 20 years, end? Why have we left the worker in the factories and offices as though the church building is the only place wherein the Holy of Holies abides?

The Catholic Labor Day Mass represented a renaissance era for the Catholic Church and the Chicago labor movement. The 1940s and 1950s were the zenith of a short-lived triumph. Both institutions were into building booms then, well-padded financial portfolios, and escalating memberships. It was a happy marriage brokered by the Association of Catholic Trade Unions, the predecessor of the Catholic Labor Alliance, and by prelates and priests like Bishop Bernard Sheil of Chicago, who interpreted papal social teaching for unionists and defended those unionists against charges of Communist influence. Since then, both the unions and the church have been through hard times; both have been bloodied and have taken survival postures.

After the 1950s the admittedly tiny Catholic movement that viewed work as a part of one's life in God left the scene.... In the 1960s the time had come for the entire church through Vatican II to address itself to being a church in the modern world, with all the unhinging of old securities that such a move would bring to its members at all levels... [And yet ironically] in the post-Vatican II church, there is, at present, no viable European or North American model for church-society rela-

> IN THE 1960S THE TIME
> had come for the entire church through Vatican II to address itself to being a church in the modern world, with all the unhinging of old securities that such a move would bring to its members at all levels...

tions, no sustained pastoral mobilization of lay energies toward world transformation, no compelling sense of the world of work as a genuine place for a religious vocation, no appropriate vision with powerful leverage to criticize the imperfections and rank injustices of the social order. The absence of these strategies and vision creates a situation of pastoral tragedy and represents a serious dereliction of duty on the part of the church. For their absence means the effective abdication of the church's vocation to transform the world.

CREATORS OF THE WORLD:
THE MEANING OF WORK AND VOCATION
by Father Dennis Geaney, OSA

I t is from the totality of our waking day with its struggles, hopes, and commitments that a vocation is gradually formed and ultimately solidly fashioned. This concept of vocation is dynamic rather than static. It is something that is always emerging and unfolding until our last breath, when we begin our enduring vocation of enjoying the endless wonders of God's beauty…

Vocation implies either an initial positive choice or the loving acceptance of what had been previously accepted with reluctance. It is an awareness of the creative possibilities of a situation and the positive desire to identify oneself with it. It is the growing realization that I can do this job, that there is a relationship between my abilities and this task. It is a decision to accept these providential circumstances, to embrace them as Christ embraced the Cross, carrying the load with external agony and inner peace.

Usually the decision is a process of growth which may not be marked by a single conscious experience of having made a choice. There may be moments of insight when the reality of the struggle is seen clearly. Ordinarily any dramatic decision that plainly marks a turn in our life is the culmination of years of minor decisions and little insights gleaned from experience. All of these pile up, waiting for the moment of truth or decision when a person solemnly declares to himself or herself that this is his work, her vocation, his niche in life, that this is the area in life in which she is going to make her contribution to the world…

God does not speak in one manner to people called to a priestly or religious vocation and in another to people called to a lay vocation. God speaks to all through their talents and their opportunities…

"I am just putting in time at work…." This statement repeated with a thousand variations in words, attitudes, and actions is implicitly a denial of the Incarnation. It is a statement of resignation from the combat in which Christ has enlisted us through Confirmation. It is a bitter defeat for the Christian personally and for the world we are called to bring to its perfection by our witness.

The statement, "I am just putting in time," is a denial of the authenticity of lay life by people who consider themselves modern apostles. It creates the image of the Catholic as a person of neurotic fears about the defilement that comes from an encounter with a most stimulating and challenging world...

To work to support a family is an act of virtue. To accept work as an expiation of sin is to show at least a partial understanding of Redemption. The Morning Offering is at least an attempt to diffuse a divine dimension into a lay or secular task.

Even with these attitudes, however, the worker may still show the fundamental disrespect for work that the desert fathers are reputed to have shown by weaving baskets in the morning which they would then unweave in the evening. Here is the same disrespect for work that teachers show for learning when they give lessons to their pupils merely to keep them busy. To offer one's work to God without any consideration of its quality or its place in the total scale of human values is to think that God acts like a thief's "fence" and asks no questions as long as the goods continued to be delivered. The Morning Offering, or a spirituality of intention, can thus sometimes be a shoddy attempt to store up divine favor for eternity with questionable gifts, as though God were interested in quantity rather than quality.

Work must be viewed positively. It is a participation in the work of creation. God left the minerals in the earth to be extracted by our labor. God left space unexplored to offer an exciting adventure after the seas, deserts, and forests had been brought under our domain. The present danger that we may abuse God's power and dangle nuclear and chemical weapons over others in a genocidal threat does not detract from the never-ceasing wonder of our partnership with God in the unfolding of creation.

God's insertion into the human race through the Incarnation gives us a part in the continuation of creation. Christ came into the world to redeem it. All of it has entered His human life—the world's beauty, its wretched misery, its defeats, its hopes. Our Lord's redemption extends beyond spiritual values. The world, the lilies of the field, bread, water, physical and spiritual blindness were all touched by Christ. Since the Incarnation, nothing but sin is foreign to the Christian. Nothing escapes the Redemption....

By the perfection of our work we are hastening the world to its fulfillment in Christ. Prayer cannot be defined as time snatched from the sordid work of the world, work which interrupts our communion with God. Prayer, rather, must be seen as the continuation of Creation, and this filling out the Body as it hastens to its fullness can only be a source of unending union with God. Every bed made, potato peeled, or ton of steel poured should be seen as

> BY THE PERFECTION
> of our work we are hastening the world to its fulfillment in Christ.

the incense of praise rising above the suburban chimney and the black clouds about the steel mill....

The car [for example] should be seen in terms of the great blessings it has brought to humankind. It has brought us to new areas where we can live away from the soot of the crowded city. It unites families scattered over the country. It brings people to see and enjoy the wonders of nature and thus affords relief from boredom.

Thus, God has called the autoworker and car salesman to be God's coworkers in helping man to establish a deeper communion with nature and a wider communion with mankind. Workers in other industries should make the effort to see how their industry fits into God's unfinished creation and how it can become the stuff of the unfolding work of Christ's redemption...

Pierre de Chardin utters the truth in almost lyrical fashion: "[God] is waiting for us at every moment in our action, in our work of the moment. [God] is in some sort at the tip of my pen, my spade, my brush, my needle—in my heart and of my thought. By pressing the stroke, the line, or the stitch on which I am engaged, to its ultimate natural finish, I shall arrive at the ultimate aim towards which my innermost will tends."

MONSIGNOR GEORGE HIGGINS

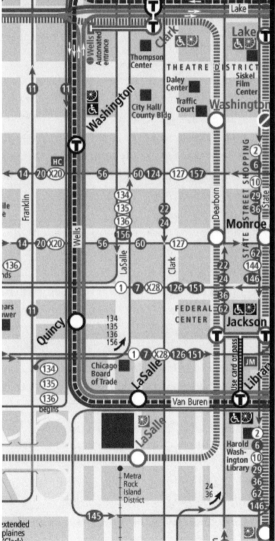

1916 - 2002

The U.S. Catholic church today is in jeopardy of losing two major constituencies. First are Mexican-American immigrants and some other new arrivals who, in tension with North American Catholicism, drift into Protestant fundamentalism or, like many in the majority culture, into secularism. Second are middle-class young adults who aspire to positions of power and responsibility and are not attracted to traditional parish and ethnic organizations. Is there anything in recent experience that might suggest principles or models for meeting the needs of these two crucial groups of workers?

Beginning in 1943, while facing the loss of a generation of working people, several priests in France and other European countries donned overalls and took full-time jobs on the docks, in mines and factories in order to present the gospel in the midst of people's daily work.

An exact counterpart of this worker-priest movement never took hold in the United States. In the 1940s through 1960s, however, a small army of U.S. Catholic clergy, known as "labor priests," served as chaplains to union locals, sat on boards of arbitration and staffed over one hundred Catholic labor schools where public skills and Catholic doctrine were taught. Monsignor George Higgins of Chicago was far and away the dean of the labor priests.

Higgins was raised in LaGrange, Illinois and ordained for the Archdiocese of Chicago in 1940. From his seminary rector Monsignor Reynold Hillenbrand and others, Higgins fully incorporated the Chicago-style of Catholicism before he moved to the nation's capital in August of 1940, where he earned a doctorate at Catholic University of America. Higgins never permanently returned to Chicago until early in 2002 when, during a talk at his boyhood parish, he fell grievously ill. He died in LaGrange, fittingly on May 1st, the feast day of Saint Joseph, the patron of all workers.

Although he was away from home, Higgins always kept in touch with the Chicago church, particularly through its gossipy "clerical grapevine." Like many of his contemporaries, Higgins was as likely to type a short note as make a phone call. (None of those featured in this book, to my knowledge, ever used e-mail, which shows how quickly technology can revolutionize pastoral practice.) A note from Higgins always concluded with the words "written in haste because I'm on my way" to Poland or California or Detroit or wherever meat cutters, miners, farm workers and other working women and men needed a friend.

Higgins was also prominent in Catholic-Jewish relations, an important player at Vatican II and an extremely well-informed journalist. In fact, he holds the record for an uninterrupted weekly newspaper column, which he titled "The Yardstick." But Higgins was best known for supporting workers, particularly through their unions.

The steady decline in membership and influence of the labor movement leads many to say that unions are a thing of the past—just another interest group. Higgins repeatedly countered this assessment, arguing that unions are an integral part of the way democratic societies ought to operate, even if for defensive reasons, that is, to keep employers afraid of a union drive. On this point Higgins often quoted Monsignor John A. Ryan of St. Paul, Minnesota: "Effective labor unions are by far the most powerful force in society for the protection of the laborer's rights and the improvement of his or her condition. No amount of employer benevolence, no diffusion of a sympathetic attitude on the part of the public, no increase of beneficial legislation, can adequately supply for the lack of organization among the workers themselves."

Unions also have a positive role to play, Higgins continued. Unions, according to Catholic social thought, are regarded as equal partners with management and government in planning the economy. Higgins called this tripartite arrangement the "Industry Council Plan." He frequently quoted Pope John XXIII's encyclical *Mater et Magistra*:

> NO AMOUNT OF EMPLOYER benevolence, no diffusion of a sympathetic attitude on the part of the public, no increase of beneficial legislation, can adequately supply for the lack of organization among the workers themselves.

"Economic order will not come naturally, simply by free competition, free enterprise and free initiative.... Intermediate bodies [like unions] are natural and necessary if we want to avoid State totalitarianism, but not for that reason alone. Institutional cooperation at all levels must be organized between the agents of the economy. Intermediate bodies must cooperate among themselves and with the government in order to help it play its positive role in the economy for the common good, national and international."

In championing "intermediate bodies," which in Catholic social thought is called the "principle of subsidiarity," Higgins was sharply critical of neo-conservatives who, though they argue for shoring up intermediate bodies like the family and churches, nonetheless show "massive and menacing lack of concern" for the decline of labor unions—among the most important mediating structures in a true democracy. "Despite their claim to be loyal to the pope," Higgins railed, "the neo-conservatives have to get off the dime and be consistent about labor unions."

My contact with Higgins was limited to an exchange of notes and articles. We crossed paths only once or twice a year at a conference or a dinner. He did graciously contribute a Foreword to Greg Pierce's and my book *Confident and Competent: A Challenge for the Lay Church* in 1987, although true to form he couldn't help but criticize the very book he was introducing. Still, he said of his objections: "These are minor points. I have raised them only to keep the dialogue going or, if you will, to keep the authors on their toes."

> ## HIGGINS AND THE OTHER
> Chicago-style leaders thought the world of work was a ripe contact point between the gospel and God's people.

On one occasion, later in his life, Higgins advised me not to take disagreements too personally. "Mature people know how to disagree," he said. Theoretically, he concluded, God's will is quite clear. But "in the give and take of a pluralistic society there are bound to be disagreements about achieving the good."

Higgins' papers are kept at Catholic University of America. The Archdiocese of Washington has instituted a "Monsignor George Higgins Award" in memory of the great labor priest. The Catholic Labor Network posts some Higgins' "Yardstick" columns on its website (www.catholiclabor.org). *George Higgins and the Quest for Worker Justice* by Father John O'Brien, CP, (Roman & Littlefield, 2005) is an extensive annotation of the "Yardstick" columns. Higgins' book, *Organized Labor and the Church* (Paulist Press, 1993), an autobiography of sorts, is still available.

Church leaders today are rightly worried about retaining young adults and newly arriving immigrants. The reference point in their talk about a solution, however, is mostly internally-oriented: how we get people involved in parish life. Higgins and the other Chicago-style leaders, on the other hand, thought the world of work was a ripe contact point between the gospel and God's people.

Will there ever be another George Higgins? Only if we look for and listen to him or her.

MISSION OF THE CHURCH
Monsignor George Higgins

I warn against the danger of oversimplifying the social mission of the post-Vatican II church and the related danger of attaching too much importance to any one ecclesiastical document on the subject of social justice....

I [offer] some random observations on what it means in a pluralistic society such as ours to combine authentic faith with contemporary relevance. In taking this tack, I do not wish in any way to denigrate the importance of the [United States bishops' pastoral letter on the economy]. I simply wish to suggest that it be kept in proper perspective lest the role of the hierarchy in carrying out the social mission of the church be overestimated and the role of the laity underestimated.

I say this because I am persuaded that, proportionately speaking, the justice and peace work of the church in the United States after Vatican II has tended to be a bit too clerical, too institutional, or, if you will, too "Churchy," for lack of a better word. Before Vatican II, paradoxically, the Catholic social action movement in the United States, though somewhat limited in scope and burdened with an inadequate, top-down type of ecclesiology, tended to emphasize more than we do today the laity's independent role, as citizens and members of secular organizations, in helping to solve social problems. At the present time, despite our greater theological awareness of the church as the "people of God," there seems to be more of a tendency to emphasize the role of Church professionals in promoting justice and defending human rights. Both approaches, of course, are valid and are usually intertwined or interrelated. There is, however, a distinction between the two, and many lay people are disappointed that the latter top-down approach is, in many cases, being more heavily emphasized after Vatican II than it was by some of the pioneers who were working in this field before the Council.

I raise this question of a "Churchy" versus secular social action because I think it has a bearing on the future of the church's involvement in the field of social justice. Is it or should it be the primary—though not exclusive—function of church-related social action organizations to prepare their members to engage in social action on their own initiative in the secular arena? Or, conversely, should it be their primary—though not exclusive—function to make sure that the institutional church and, more specifically, the ecclesiastical hierarchy, is publicly committed to the cause of social justice? This strikes me as being a timely question and one that ought to be given careful consideration in any reexamination of the impact of Vatican II.

> THERE IS A NEED TO REVIEW our justice and peace policies and programs at every level to make sure that they are adequately oriented toward forming authentic and autonomous lay leaders who will exercise their apostolate, not in and through church organizations, but in their secular occupations.

It could also be argued, I think, that many of the people involved in social action causes before Vatican II saw more clearly than some of today's activists the distinction between "activism" and social action. Some of the latter tend to put perhaps too much stock in the advocacy of this or that form of prophetic witness and are perceived as not being sufficiently interested in promoting long-range programs of social education and structural reform that do not produce measurable results in the short run.

Under this same heading, I think we must be prepared to listen to those members of the laity who think that—again, proportionately speaking—the church in the United States is devoting a lot of time, energy and money to training and feeding Church professionals, both clerical and lay, and insufficient time, energy and money to programs aimed at helping lay people prepare themselves to play their own autonomous role as Christians in the temporal order.

I think it would be a mistake, of course, for the church to get bogged down at this time in an academic, theoretical debate about the respective roles of the laity and of Church professionals in the field of social justice. Theologians can, should and undoubtedly will continue to grapple with this question at their leisure. It would probably be an even greater mistake to draw too sharp a distinction at the practical level—as the Holy Father [Pope John Paul II] himself has been accused of doing—between the role of the laity and the role of the clergy in promoting justice and defending human rights. At the same time, however, there is a need,

I think, to review our justice and peace policies and programs at every level to prevent them from becoming top-heavy with Church professionals or, in more positive terms, to make sure that they are adequately oriented toward forming authentic and autonomous lay leaders who will exercise their apostolate, not in and through church organizations, but in their secular occupations.

THE ACT OF SOCIAL JUSTICE IS ORGANIZING
Monsignor George G. Higgins

The virtue of social justice is easy to talk about but difficult to define, and even more difficult to put into practice.

What is social justice? Pope Pius XI refers to it as that virtue which demands "from each individual all that is necessary for the common good." A big order, to be sure, and one that even the best of Catholics, without any noticeable twinge of conscience, can rather habitually fail to carry out.

Father William Ferree, SM, in *The Act of Social Justice* wrote by far the best and most original North American study on the nature and practice of this most important virtue.

> ## THERE ARE THOSE WHO
> are so "impressed by the great mass of social disorder and the difficulty of reform," that "they consider that responsibility can apply to personal life only."

"Now leaving out the men of ill will, including the indifferent and the lazy," he asks, to our embarrassment, "what men of good will are rather habitual offenders against social justice despite *their good intentions*?"

First of all, he replies, there are those who are so "impressed by the great mass of social disorder and the difficulty of reform," that "they consider that responsibility can apply to personal life only." Far from being a virtue, Ferree says, this attitude (which, often enough, is only a cover-up for cynicism) is "a sin against social justice because it abdicates leadership in the very institutions which it itself perpetuates by its participation."

Different illustrations of this all too often failing will naturally suggest themselves to different readers. The following are offered only as typical examples: Refusal to participate in union affairs because the union happens to be temporarily under the control of undesirable leadership—and besides, the argument continues, if people would only be decent, we wouldn't need to have unions. Refusal to vote in political elections on the ground that political life is hopelessly corrupt. Opposition to the United States on the theory that, unless and until all men return to God and to the moral law, there can be no hope of peace. An attitude of apathy and indifference about social and economic legislation based on the excuse that you can't change attitudes by means of legislation.

Secondly, Father Ferree continues, there are those who "add to the lack of solidarity (social charity) of the former class (the abdicators), a lack of appreciation also for the very complexity of life which so impresses these former. While thus tragically simplifying the problem of responsibility to individual means only, they throw the whole crushing weight of social disorder upon unsupported and isolated individual consciences and upon personal heroism in resisting evil."

And finally there are those who disdain the tedious and thankless work of organization itself, not necessarily because they are lazy, but because they look upon organization "as somehow below their dignity

> # TOO OFTEN PEOPLE SAY,
> "Let George do it," while they indulge in the comforting luxury of telling George by hindsight that he should have done it differently.

or wasteful of their time." Among the worst offenders in this regard, according to Father Ferree, are some who have been blessed with the advantages of a better-than-average education and who, for that very reason, might reasonably be expected to make a better-than-average contribution to the cause of social justice. Too often, instead they say, "Let George do it," while they indulge in the comforting luxury of telling George by hindsight that he should have done it differently.

If Father Ferree is unimpressed by our "good intentions" in the face of our frequent failure to do "all that is necessary for the common good" (which means our failure to correct the bad economic and social institutions to which we belong, or to organize good institutions where needed), he is in the best of company. He is merely re-echoing the authoritative opinion of the saintly Pope Pius X who told us long ago:

Catholic Action will not please certain timid souls who, though good living, are so attached to their habitual quiet and so afraid of every innovation that they believe that it is quite sufficient to pray, because God knows best how to defend the faith and humiliate His enemies and make the church triumphant. But these good people…will wait in vain for society to re-Christianize itself simply by their prayers…. It is necessary to join prayers with action…. There are others, on the other hand, who, in order to justify their inertia, give the world up for lost, since they see in it so many evils."

Was Pius X talking about us?

A WARNING FROM CHICAGO
Monsignor George G. Higgins

The highly praised *Chicago Declaration of Christian Concern*, a statement issued in 1977 by a group of Chicago area Catholics [and reprinted in this book], warned that the Catholic church may have lost a generation of lay leadership because of its preoccupation since Vatican II with internal "Churchy" affairs and its consequent devaluation of the laity's social responsibility.

In particular, the statement pointed to three recent developments among American Catholics. The first was the movement to involve lay persons in the Church's official ministries; this had the ironic effect of drawing attention away from the secular mission of the laity. The second was the tendency of some clergy members to preempt the role of lay Catholics in social reform. The third was a trend of diminishing interest in Christian social thought as the mediating ground between the gospel and specific political and economic issues...

Drafters of the *Chicago Declaration* wait "impatiently for a new prophecy, a new word that can once again stir the laity to see the grandeur of the Christian vision for man in society and move priests to galvanize lay persons in their secular-religious role." They point out that in the final analysis, "the church speaks to and acts upon the world through her laity.... Without a dynamic laity conscious of its ministry to the world, the church in effect does not speak or act." The Chicago group added: "It would be one of the great ironies of history if the era of Vatican II which opened the windows of the church to the world were to close with the church turned upon herself."

Ecclesiastical chauvinism has no more to recommend it than civil national super-patriotism. This is by way of saying that a Chicago priest ought to have enough common sense to avoid boasting about his own city or his own archdiocese. Bearing this caution in mind, I will risk saying that the informal committee of Chicago priests, sisters, bothers, and lay people—in their call for "a reexamination of present tendencies in the church," in hope of "a new sense of direction"— performed a very useful service to the U.S. Catholic community.

This is not to suggest, nor do its signers pretend, that the *Chicago Declaration* had the last word on the subject. It did, however, raise many of the right questions. The group's purpose was not to try to answer these questions once and for all but to start a serious dialogue about them among fellow-Catholics not only in Chicago but throughout the nation.

> ## CLERICS HAVE NO MONOPOLY
> on the new forms of clericalism criticized by the *Chicago Declaration*.

That much it did, at least to some extent, even if the issues pressed by the *Chicago Declaration* have never made it to the top of the church's agenda in the United States. To add a few remarks to the conversation, I would begin by suggesting that the *Chicago Declaration*—to which, in the main, I fully subscribe—may have drawn too sharp a distinction between the respective roles of the laity and the clergy in the social ministry of the church. Those who drafted the statement expressed concern that the absence of lay initiative may take us down the road to a new form of clericalism. If this happens, they suggest, the blame would go to many priests, sisters and brothers who "have bypassed the laity to pursue social concerns of their own [and] have sought to impose their own agenda for the world upon the laity."

The point is well taken, but I believe the late great German theologian, Father Karl Rahner, SJ, came closer to the truth when he observed that clerics have no monopoly on the new forms of clericalism criticized by the *Chicago Declaration*. Rahner pointed out that "the same fault, but with the sign reversed, is probably met with just as often among the laity (or among clerics with lay mentality)... How many times have we read editorials by lay Catholic journalists who set up a problem—say, famine in sub-Sahara Africa—and then rush to the question: What are the bishops going to do about it? To me, however, a more important question is: What are we, the whole church, "the people of God," going to do about it? Rahner describes these lay people as "lay defeatists."

Rahner did not say that clergy should withdraw from the church's social ministry. He said that clergy zeal for social reform, admirable in itself, out to be coupled with a sense of realism. Clergy should realize that they don't have all the answers to all complicated problems confronting the modern world. The laity should not expect them to provide such answers. More profoundly, Rahner argued that the Church and the church's ministry are not exactly the same. He wrote, "The limits of the church's possibilities and those of its official hierarchy are not to be regarded form the outset as identical."

In substance, the *Chicago Declaration* says the same thing. But Rahner has gone a step further by reminding us that clericalism or clerical triumphalism presents a somewhat more complicated problem than the *Chicago Declaration* would suggest. In other words, it is not simply a matter of clergy and religious usurping the role of the laity.

In the late 1980s, the debate resurfaced as bishops around the world gathered for a synod in Rome to address the role of the laity (in all spheres of church and social life). Articles, pamphlets, meetings and at least one book offered a fresh look at the *Chicago Declaration*. William Droel and Gregory Pierce, in their 1987 book *Confident and Competent: A Challenge for the Lay Church*, provided an extended commentary and elaboration on the *Chicago Declaration's* themes. The authors did not sign the *Chicago Declaration*, nor were they involved in the consultation leading up to it. Yet they agreed with the statement's thrust and, on the basis of their own experience and in light of subsequent developments, attempted to flesh it out, so to speak, and bring it up to date. They did so convincingly, and in view of the fact that the 1987 synod in Rome dealt with the laity's role, their timing was perfect.

I suggest however, that while we need such books what we need more is the living example of lay-initiated programs based on the principles of the *Chicago Declaration*. The laity have a right to expect the so-called "official" Church to respect these principles and to help the laity put them into practice. Droel and Pierce correctly cite "a tremendous need for programs to support the laity in their vocation to job, family and neighborhood." Experience suggests, however, that lay initiative in developing programs of this type is indispensable.

To spend too much time theorizing about the laity's role or lamenting the failure of official Church leaders to deal with the problem is to sell the laity short or, worse, to encourage a new form of clericalism, or "lay defeatism." This is not to say that the drafters of the *Chicago Declaration* fell into this trap. To the contrary, they have played an indispensable role in clarifying the mission of lay Catholics.

It would be a mistake, however, to think that statements alone will bring about the changes that they have rightly called for. In short, the time has come for a new burst of lay-initiated action of the type, if I may say, that brought a fleeting measure of fame to Chicago-style Catholicism in the 1940s and 1950s.

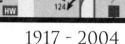

ED MARCINIAK

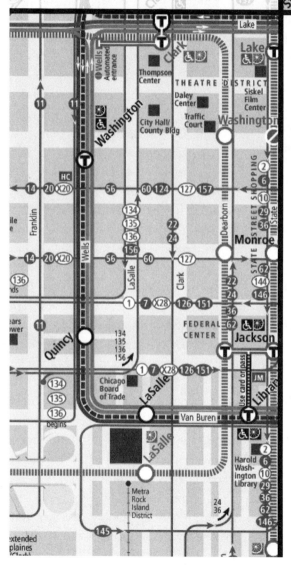

1917 - 2004

xcept during his last days, Ed Marciniak phoned me almost every day for the last twenty-two or more years of his life. (Yes, including Saturday morning. Yes, sometimes on Sunday evening.) All of the calls were quite short, but each contained an implicit request, really more like an order. Very often Marciniak was trying to help someone and needed information. "A religious order is busting a union of janitors at such-and-such hospital," he might begin. "Do we know anyone in that order who can give us the inside story?" Or it might be a grammar school that needed money or a community group that needed allies.

Many times I suspected Marciniak already knew the answer to his question but was calling just to keep me in the conversation or get me thinking. "Jack Egan wants to quote something from Jacques Maritain," a typical call would begin. "Do you have any books by Maritain?" I would hang up, thinking, "Why would Egan and Marciniak, who actually knew the legendary French philosopher, call me about some quotation?" Yet, by-and-by, I would look in my library for Maritain books. If I found them, I would peruse them for a pertinent quote. If I had no such books, I would make it a point to buy them, figuring that if they were good enough for Egan and Marciniak they were required reading for me.

> THANKS TO MARCINIAK
> and his friends, the word *Catholic*
> became part of the history of the U.S.
> labor movement, especially in Chicago.

As best I can remember, I was first introduced to Marciniak in the early 1980s at a National Center for the Laity conference on Pope John Paul II's encyclical *On Human Work*. Marciniak was disturbed that in a nation of over 50 million Catholics, only 10,000 copies of the encyclical had been printed. How did he know? Like with other topics, Marciniak did his research. He called all the Catholic publishers to find out their print runs, scolding them while he had them on the line.

Marciniak started a Catholic Worker house in Chicago in 1938. With John Cogley, he began publishing the *Chicago Catholic Worker* in June of that year. The circulation of the Chicago paper grew rapidly and got national attention when it attacked Father Charles Coughlin, the famous radio priest, for his anti-Semitism. On March 19, 1943 (the feast of St. Joseph, the patron saint of workers), Marciniak, with Monsignor Reynold Hillenbrand and Frank Delaney, founded the Catholic Labor Alliance, later known as the Council for Working Life. Through it he published *Work* newspaper and *New City* magazine.

Marciniak was responsible for making the Catholic Worker movement and related organizations a force in the industrial union movement. Thanks to Marciniak and his friends, the word *Catholic* became part of the history of the U.S. labor movement, especially in Chicago. Imagine that today.

Like the other disciples of Hillenbrand, Marciniak simply assumed that Catholic social principles as articulated in the encyclicals and other church documents could be applied with evident benefit to labor relations, race relations, social policy and urban affairs. He taught many classes based on the encyclicals, including at Dominican University in River Forest, Illinois, (then called Rosary College), where a prominent businessman threatened to withhold a major donation unless the college fired "that Catholic communist, Ed the Red." (The Dominican Sisters took a financial loss and an integrity gain by backing Marciniak.)

Marciniak argued that Catholics should be active in unions as good trade unionists who happen to be Catholic or as business leaders in professional associations who happen to be Catholic, not as Catholics representing the Church. The good trade unionist is "careful not to involve the Church per se in the temporal problems of the union," he wrote. (Marciniak capitalized *Church* when it referred exclusively to the institutional Church and kept it lower case when *church* meant *people of God*.)

Policies are Catholic because they are true and good, Marciniak argued, not because they are Catholic. Understanding this distinction, he wrote, "will determine in great measure the amount of influence that Catholic labor groups and indeed the whole Catholic social movement will exert."

He also felt that while it may be worthwhile to have a Catholic support group for lawyers, nurses or neighbors, for example, when it comes to advocating public policies, those same lawyers, nurses or neighbors would be better advised to act inside their professional association, union, community organization or political party rather than through a specifically Catholic peace and justice organization.

Likewise Marciniak felt it is impossible to go directly from Scripture or Church documents to specific social policies. Catholics and others must use common sense and prudential judgment when crafting legislation, designing hospital policies, and completing all other public tasks. Marciniak liked to tell about G.K. Chesterton's response to the question: What book would you most like if you were stranded on a deserted island? "I'd like the *Idiot's Guide to Shipbuilding*, not the Bible," Chesterton replied.

These distinctions put Marciniak into conflict, sharply on occasion, with Church employees who gave opinions on specific public policies, often quoting Scripture or a Church document, as if they were speaking for the whole church or the entire diocese. Those Church employees, Marciniak felt, are unwittingly undermining the responsibility of all baptized Christians.

During the 1950s and 1960s Marciniak was deeply involved in improving race relations. He was active in the Catholic Interracial Council in Chicago, a founder of the National Catholic Conference on Interracial Justice, and a cofounder of the National Catholic Social Action Conference. He was also the head of the Chicago Commission on Human Relations, beginning in 1960, under the original Mayor Richard Daley. (He was sometimes criticized for working for Daley, especially during a time of racial tension in Chicago, but this fit in well with Marciniak's belief that more change is made by those "inside" the institutions of society than by "outside" social justice efforts.)

Marciniak became president of the National Center for Urban Ethnic Affairs in 1984, succeeding Monsignor Geno Baroni, and for many years he was president of the Institute for Urban Life at Loyola University, Chicago.

Marciniak died in 2004, almost ten years after his beloved wife Virginia, who was his partner in every way. His papers are kept at the Archdiocese of Chicago Bernardin Archives and Records Center. Some of his publications are available through the National Center for the Laity.

No one embodied Church, Chicago-style more than Ed Marciniak. He was a burr under the saddle of everyone and anyone who tried to rationalize inaction or ineffective action, especially in the name of religion…or the church he loved.

BEING A CHRISTIAN IN THE WORLD OF WORK
by Ed Marciniak

I n his 1981 encyclical *On Human Work*, Pope John Paul II had no modest purpose in mind. He invited each of us to consider the idea of a new civilization based on the spirituality of work. For him work is "at the very center of the *social question*." He proposed a work ethic which would give labor priority over capital—whether that capital was owned by the state or by private investors. Are such ideas too radical for America?

Monsignor George Higgins, who now teaches at Catholic University, noted that the encyclical was "a more radical document than it has been portrayed." Why is it radical? Because, Higgins explains, "it calls for a complete re-examination of the world's political and economic structures."

Terry Herndon, executive director of the National Education Association, said that for him "the most compelling single statement in the document is the ringing affirmation that the value of work is determined not by the kind of work being done but by the fact that the one doing it is a person."

> JOHN PAUL II
> invited each of us to consider the idea of a new civilization based on the spirituality of work.

Author Malachi Martin called the encyclical "radical" because "with one clean stroke, John Paul II...severed the economic chain that has shackled Christendom to capitalism since capitalism was born in the West. Deliberately, without trace of waffle, he has junked this hoary alliance and reaffirmed the original bond between the church and the worker." John Paul II, Martin says, "anticipates a society that has never been—not capitalist in any known guise, but emphatically not socialist."

That view was echoed by Arthur Jones, a columnist for the *National Catholic Reporter* who said the pope was taking a "third way—neither capitalist nor Marxist nor halfway between."

John Paul II does not seem to be proposing some new socio-economic order as an alternative to existing systems. He has no blueprint. Instead he is offering a way of looking at and evaluating any economic arrangement, however primitive or technological, to determine how it can enhance the dignity of the worker. Consequently the civilization he foresees is not based on that leisure which relies upon escapist entertainment or the commercial and advertising vices associated with the mass media; nor does it originate in the high culture associated with Ivy League universities and traditional wealth.

> USE YOUR IMAGINATION.
> Exploit your ingenuity. Puzzle out what in the workaday world needs changing—and then do it!

Audaciously, John Paul II presents us with his "gospel of work," with his reflections, for example, on the "scourge of unemployment," the devaluation of the work of mothers, the importance of labor unions, the impact of automation and a dozen other topics—in sum, his vision of a new civilization.

For John Paul II the worker may be a farmer, miner, factory wage earner, professional person, soldier, civil servant, entrepreneur or executive. The worker may don a blue collar or white collar—or wear no shirt at all. The work done may be in the home or outside it. All are workers.

John Paul II's letter is not primarily about business ethics or about morals in the marketplace. The question to which he asks us to respond is larger, on the one hand, and more personal on the other. How can a social and economic system best serve workers, their children and grandchildren? How can it enhance the meaning and dignity of work? How can it reach the ideal described by St. Irenaeus: "The glory of God is man fully alive."

John Paul II challenges not only North Americans, and those in other developed nations like Japan, the Soviet Union, Germany, and Israel, but also those who work in developing countries like India, Mexico, Vietnam, Haiti, China, Lebanon, and Nigeria. John Paul II's appeal is directed to everybody—to those where state capitalism is installed, to those where private capital dominates, and to those where capital is scarce and the laborers legion.

Written as a pastoral letter, *On Human Work* will discourage the age-old habits of "encyclical thwacking"—as practiced by Catholic militants of the left or right who enjoy whacking their ideological opponents with a selected quotation from a papal encyclical or some oft-spoken bishop. The encyclical is conciliatory in tone, not condemnatory. Free of dogmatism, it seeks to persuade and convince. It calls upon Christians to regard their work as sharing in God's own creative work....

Allow me to paraphrase what John Paul II is saying to us in my own vernacular: Don't ask me for a blueprint. I don't have one. Don't ask me to spell it out for you. That's your job. Mine is to be provocative, to be challenging, to remind you about the dignity of work and how human rights are being violated. For God's sake and your own, use your imagination. Exploit your ingenuity. Puzzle out what in the workaday world needs changing—and then do it!

What stands between the rhetoric and the reality? On the one hand, there is John Paul II's vision of a society giving primacy to human work; and on the other hand, there is the reality of a world whose countries differ in their stages of economic development, whose political systems range from democratic to despotic, whose peoples are overwhelmed by the surge of sudden wealth or by centuries of primitive poverty. In the ideal world, how is the "gospel of work" to be incarnated?

To stand on Mount Pisgah and enjoy the vision of the Promised Land is not the same as reaching it. Bridges have to be erected, roads built, food grown and stored, and enemies placated. Inertia has to be overcome and hope offered to the helpless.

Focusing only on the United States, I must admit that the roadway from John Paul II's rhetoric to the realization is already lined with roadblocks and detours inherited from the past. Have you not heard it said: "What does a Polish-born pope know about the U.S. economic system?" Does his worldview indeed choke off the free market, reduce individual incentive and socialize the means of production? Will anyone take him seriously? Will those who present his ideas for a Christian spirituality of work and try to adapt it in the North American scene be laughed off the nation's stage?

These are not impertinent questions. In a nation of 50 million Catholics, the U.S. Conference of Catholic Bishops printed 20,000 copies of *On Human*

Work. Having sold out the first edition, the publication staff is considering a new printing of "5,000 or 10,000 copies." Is the new press run a vote of confidence or not? This weekend the National Religion and Labor Conference convenes in Milwaukee and the encyclical topic or something resembling its major theme cannot be found on the program.

There are other straws in the wind. *On Human Work* has had an impact on some North American bishops. It has revived their interest in celebrating Labor Day. Last month the bishops were asked to commemorate Labor Day by pondering *On Human Work* and by praying for a reduction in unemployment. In writing to his fellow bishops, Bishop Mark J. Hurley of Santa Rosa, California, chair of the bishop's Committee on Social Development and World Peace said: "It is especially appropriate for the church to use this national holiday…to call attention to the dignity of work." Since the traditional Labor Day Mass has been disappearing over the last two decades, we now have an indicator that will assess how seriously John Paul II's encyclical is being taken by Catholics across the continent. On Labor Day this year I will tally the dioceses which take up Bishop Hurley's suggestion….

To begin a dialogue on Christianity in the world of work, I propose a five-point agenda:

1. More denizens of the world of work will have to find a Christian vocation in their work.

Many Christians, whatever their occupation or profession, prefer to keep their Sunday religion separate from their work-filled weekdays. They would just as soon have the ordained minister handle the sacred work of worship on Sunday while they busy themselves with family and secular work the rest of the week. Only on Sunday are they accustomed to confronting the Gospel personally. Their orientation is toward a career, not a vocation.

The vote for such a point of view, however, is by no means unanimous. Sen. Mark Hatfield (R-Org.), for example, belongs to a prayer group of long standing on Capitol Hill. The group is ecumenical comprising Baptist, Presbyterian, Methodist, and Catholic senators. They are not members of the New Right; they have been meeting and praying together long before the Moral Majority arrived in Washington. Why do they gather together in Christ's name? Sen. Hatfield answers that we need to know "where we are between Sundays.... We are the church dispersed in the world." When he wrote a book on his Senate experience of managing Christian values and public issues he titled it, fittingly enough, *Between a Rock and a Hard Place*.

Sen. Hatfield is not alone. Throughout the land there indeed are a great many workers who want to behave as Christians seven days a week, not just on Sunday. May their tribe increase.

> THROUGHOUT THE LAND there indeed are a great many workers who want to behave as Christians seven days a week, not just on Sunday.

2. Clearer signals will have to be sent to the Christian laity with regard to secular and sacred pathways to God, to holiness.

Among many Church leaders and their staffs there lingers an abiding disdain for those Christians who work inside the political and economic system and a predilection for those who are stationed outside or against the system. Many of the Church's civil servants (priests, religious and laity who are full-timers in the parish, diocesan office or the church-related hospital or school) operate with a built-in bias. From the periphery of economic and political institutions they tend to stand in judgment and condemnations, not knowing how to commend, encourage or support the insiders, those businessmen professional women and men, union leaders, who are persons of integrity and allergic to injustice.

Some recent experiences illustrate the confusion, the lack of understanding that prevails about the way Christians go about carrying out their vocation inside government, labor unions, hospitals, military academies, schools, factories, offices, trade and professional associations, or multinational corporations.

A Christian businessman I know was invited to a conference sponsored by a divinity school. When he arrived, the students and faculty pounced on him—insisting that he immediately endorse their proposals for carrying out his corporation's social responsibility. He listened attentively and patiently. But after being preached at for nearly an hour, the businessman finally exploded, reminding his clerical hosts: "What makes you think that you know more about business ethics, more about solving the ethical riddles of a corporation than I do? That's my job

five and six days a week. For you, it's an avocation. For me, it's my full-time vocation. I'm not perfect. That's why I accepted your invitation. But please give me
some credit for trying to do an honest-to-God job, as I do for your calling."

Notre Dame Magazine recently published an article saluting nine U.S. senators and representatives who had brought honor to their calling. The editor then
vitiated the article's thrust by adding a caption that the U.S. Congress was "filled
with hacks and timeservers." The issue is not the accuracy of this glittering gener-
ality but the attitude which let it be printed. It was the editor's predisposition that
is at the heart of the matter: the readiness to belittle political insiders.

Seeking to justify his refusal to vote in a hotly contested local election, a parish priest in Chicago not long ago dismissed the two political rivals, whom he did
not know at all as venal, saying: "What's the difference? One politician smokes a
long cigar; the other, a short one." His attitude is not surprising when you recall
that most of the saints canonized by the Catholic Church have been men and
women who withdrew from the world. It was this practice that prompted Martin
Luther to charge that the real saints were those who put up with squalling infants,
shrewish wives and drunken husbands.

In a recent survey of 1,100 professors at Christian seminaries and schools
of theology, 70 percent of them thought that business leaders as a rule paid little
or no attention "to religious values in making decisions for their companies." The
theological faculty's opinion of politicians was somewhat better. Only 37 percent
of the professors were convinced that politicians as a rule paid little or no attention "to religious values in making public decisions." Once again I must ask: What
nourishes the attitude that leads to such mean-spirited conclusions? Is it a reluctance to recognize the Christian spirituality of work and to appreciate that truck
farmers, electricians, politicians, homemakers, nurses and janitors are called to
holiness through their daily chores?

The tension between the sacred and secular passageways to God received
high visibility in the Oscar-winning movie *Chariots of Fire*. The film is based on
actual events. Eric Liddell, a senior at Edinburgh University, delays taking up his
vocation as a missionary to run the 400 meters in the 1924 Olympics in Paris. His
sister insists that his missionary work in China is more important. The Flying
Scotsman tries to explain to her that "his talent for running is a gift from God,

which he must not spurn. He will be able to go on with his missionary work only if, at whatever pain to his family, he serves God in his own way"—by sprinting in the Olympic games. "When I run," Liddell says, "I can feel his pleasure." Of course athletic prowess, like work, can be transformed into prayer.

3. Special ministries to serve working women and men will have to be organized.

Despite the explosions of ministries in the Church, conspicuously absent are ministries directed to the millions of Christians in secular jobs. Examine the content of diocesan religious education anywhere,

> DESPITE THE EXPLOSION of ministries in the Church, conspicuously absent are ministries directed to the millions of Christians in secular jobs.

the curriculum of any seminary or theological school, or the emphasis of almost any elementary parish program. You will find that those enrolled are indeed being educated, but educated for paid or volunteer positions within the Church. What happened to the world of work which so concerns John Paul II?

In surveying the U.S. scene, Cardinal Joseph Bernardin recently concluded that "despite today's enormously increased interest in lay ministry, I am convinced that we have scarcely begun to tap its rich potential. Bearing in mind that the primary field for the exercise of lay ministry is in the workaday world, its possibilities within the church are vast…. The laity's specific role is not to serve the Church in an institutional sense, but the world. In virtue of their baptism and confirmation, they share in Christ's priesthood and are charged with the responsibility of bringing the message of the Gospel to the world."

As lay ministries continue to multiply, will Christians find the opportunity to engage in sustained discussion and reflection on topics such as the following?

Colman McCarthy, a syndicated columnist and a former editorial writer for *The Washington Post*, said: "Both the church and the world need saints in the marketplace. We've proved we can run orphanages and soup kitchens. But we haven't proved we can run AT & T's, the General Motors, the Merchandise Marts."

Raymond Kroc, founder of McDonald's, expressed himself this way: "I speak of faith in McDonald's as if it were a religion. I believe in God, family and

McDonald's—and in the office, this order is reversed."

The international operatic superstar, Luciano Pavarotti, put his personal philosophy into these words: "The voice is a gift God has given to everybody and to kick myself to make it the best.... Opera has given me a lot. It is time to give something back."

John Caron, president of Caron International, a yarn manufacturing company which has 2,000 employees in six plants, four in the United States and others in Belgium and Holland, has been asked this question a thousand times: Can you really be a Christian in today's business world? Caron always replies: "There's only one answer. You have to be, if your religion means anything to you." Caron laments: "Students with whom I talk think that business decisions are all black and white. That's not true at all. There's always a mixture of good and bad in every alternative, and you have to ask yourself which outweighs the other."

Georgia Anne Geyer another newspaper columnist, recently reported on a television show in which an elderly black woman spoke of her classroom teaching: "This is my work, my blessing, not my doom." The show then depicted three students who, though without experience, announced staunchly that they would accept only certain high-level types of work. Geyer reacted: "Allow me a personal note. By these three young people's standards, I have no 'pride' at all. In my student days I was ecstatic to work as a waitress. I used to go to downtown Chicago one day a week from Northwestern University to do petty office work. I worked until 2 a.m. at the college newspaper, doing the grimiest jobs. And when I started my adult career I went joyously form being a society reporter (something a 'liberated' woman like myself should have hated!) to being a street reporter, to being a foreign correspondent, to being a columnist." She concluded by saying it was impossible to "want to *be* without *doing*.... That's what the work ethic is about—nobody's going anywhere without it."

Each of the above quotations represents the point of view of well-known people about the spirituality of work. However, the same topics are discussed all the time around kitchen tables, during coffee breaks, on the lunch hour or in the local bar; only the discussants are ordinary women and men. Where a Christian work ethic is seldom debated or fostered is within the Church's schools, adult education programs, discussion groups and homilies.

4. The language of those who stress the Christian spirituality of work will have to be updated.

How do modern Christians communicate with each other about the holiness to be found at the workbench, behind a tractor, at a typewriter or beside a hospital bed? If sanctity is not locked up in the rectory or monastery, how is it sought in a bank or office? In preparing this talk I benefited from the reaction of many friends. Some argued that in singling out spirituality, holiness and sanctity, I was mouthing banalities and platitudes.

What then is the appropriate language to explain and proclaim the "gospel of work?" E.F. Schumacher found the right words in his books on work and holiness: *Small Is Beautiful,*

> HOW DO MODERN
> Christians communicate with each other about the holiness to be found at the workbench, behind a tractor, at a typewriter or beside a hospital bed?

Guide for the Perplexed and *Good Work,* which were read and enjoyed by millions. In their struggle for freedom Polish workers have invested "solidarity" with new human and religious significance. In reviewing the film *Chariots of Fire*, Stanley Kauffmann, the movie critic for *The New Republic* praised the film for being "inspiriting without being inspirational." For me that word "inspiriting" resounds with meaning. The liberating elements of work are still appreciated, as are the dignity and integrity of work well done.

Not long ago the *Chicago Tribune* featured a letter which chastised its journalists for using such "derogatory terms" as "non-working wife" and "non-working mother." The work of the so-called "non-working mother," the writer claimed, "is more essential to the well-being of our society than are most of the 20,000 jobs listed in the Dictionary of Occupational Titles.... Of course, if our society acknowledged the worth and dignity of every person, regardless of the job and acknowledged the dignity of all honest work no matter how menial, then the above comments would not be necessary."

The interest in "making" a retreat, certainly a traditionally Christian experience, has now been appropriated by business, industry and social welfare agencies to describe a weekend where a group of workers gathers to reflect on how well they are carrying out their work so that they can plan for the future. Has "retreat" been secularized? Yes, but not totally irreversibly.

Some have suggested that the deficiency is not in the outmoded language we use but in the absence of a genuinely North American theology of work. If we had that theology, some argue, it would be fleshed out with words of meaning. Who is willing to develop a theology for Martha?

Dorothy L. Sayers, the writer of mystery fiction and the creator of Lord Peter Whimsey, a detective who was good at his job, wrote: "In nothing has the Church so lost her hold on the laity as in her failure to understand and respect secular vocation. She has allowed work and religion to become separate departments and is astonished to find that, as a result, the secular work of the world is turned to purely selfish and destructive ends, and that the greater part of the world's intelligent workers have become irreligious, or at least, uninterested in religion. But is it astonishing? How can anyone remain interested in a religion which seems to have no concern with nine-tenths of life?

> TO RAISE THE LIVING
> standards for those at the bottom, economic development and growth are indispensable.

"The Church's approach to an intelligent carpenter is usually confined to exhorting him not to be drunk and disorderly in his leisure hours, to come to church on Sundays. What the Church should be telling him is this: that the very first demand that his religion makes upon him is that he should make good tables. Church, by all means, and decent forms of amusement, certainly—but what use is all of that if in the very center of his life and occupation he is insulting God with bad carpentry...? No piety in the worker will compensate for work that is not true to itself; for any work that is untrue to its own technique is a living lie."

5. Christian discussions of wealth and poverty, of the virtues associated with just distribution, will have to cease edging out the virtues of work, service and production.

To raise the living standards for those at the bottom, economic development and growth are indispensable. A rising tide, as the saying goes, raises all boats.

The parent who prepares meals for the family; the hard-working farmers whose skills enable them to grow more and better wheat and rice; the government official or private entrepreneur who surmounts natural and man-made obstacles to provide pure water or electricity to an underdeveloped region makes major advances in the cause of social justice. Those who focus their concerns solely on the distribution of resources or on the contrasts between rich and poor, neglect development—economic, social and personal.

Risking oversimplification, I conclude that outsiders to the social and economic system press for a more just distribution of the resources which God entrusted to us. On the other hand, the insiders, who appreciate better how a social and economic institution functions and how it can be harnessed to perform better and to be more just, see such an institution as an engine of change.

The other weakness of the distribution strategy by itself is that it seeks to plant the seeds of guilt. Such a strategy, however, has a motivation span far shorter than those who use it realize.

When one seeks to uproot poverty, for example, one can stress the misery of the lowly to excite the compassion of the mighty. But in the long run the strategy that works relies on the experience of those who actually made it out of poverty, who moved into the mainstream. When we ask, "How did they do it?" we are pointing to the virtues of work, service and achievement.

Robert Greenleaf, a business executive, said that the course of his life was changed by a college professor who told his class that the large institutions which dominate society—government, union, business, the universities—were not serving the public well: "You can do as I do, stand outside and criticize, bring pressure if you can, write and argue about it. All of this may do some good. But nothing of substance will happen unless there are people inside these institutions who are able to (and want to) lead them into better performance for the public good." Greenleaf chose to work from the inside.

John Paul's letter *On Human Work* was well timed. In the United States the world of work, the realm of the insider, is changing profoundly. Some say explosively. Inexorably the U.S. social and economic system is being transformed from an industrial to a service economy. The statistics are not that unfamiliar.

Today it takes only 3 percent of the workers to feed the country and export huge grain surpluses. In 1900, 70 percent of the workers were engaged in the production of goods. Today less than 30 percent are so employed. The other 70 percent are employed in service occupations. These are health, education, law and communications; public utilities and transportation; wholesale and retail trade, finance, insurance, and real estate; government; and other services such as hotels, restaurants and repair shops. The largest single "industry," without a serious competitor, is health care. It absorbs $275 billion annually. In 1982 McDonald's, the fast food chain, employed twice as many people as did the U.S. Steel Corp.

During the present recession, significantly, the service industries have actually been hiring additional workers. Unemployment has been concentrated in the goods-producing industries, such as steel, auto, and homebuilding. This is not a new trend.

The growing presence of women in the nation's labor force outside the home has been even more spectacular. In 1980, 43 percent of the workers were women, up from 29 percent in 1950. By 1990 the majority of all workers are expected to be women. In 1981 the U.S. Bureau of Labor Statistics reported that 58 percent of all mothers with children under 18 were employed outside the home. Millions of these children live in single-parent families. Twenty-six million of all children had working mothers at home, while 32 million had mothers working elsewhere.

The world of work in the United States is being radically altered. The transformation is having a near-revolutionary impact upon family, neighborhood and church. The center of gravity in our society is shifting even as we ponder John Paul's letter on work.

More than a century ago John Stuart Mill said: "No great improvements in the lot of mankind are possible, until a great change takes place in the fundamental constitutions of their modes of thought." It was the same wisdom, I believe, that moved Pope John Paul II to deepen the dialogue on human work. We in North America do need a theology of work or, if you prefer, philosophy of labor. We are being challenged to develop a Christian spirituality of work to cope with the economic and social changes that have already arrived and with those that are yet to come.

To borrow a sports metaphor, the ball is in our court. The initiative is ours.

WE NEED ACTION
Ed Marciniak

While in Washington not long ago, I met with friends, one of whom, Bob Senser, had just returned from Bangladesh. While there he had interviewed garment workers, mostly women, as well as two girls, ages eight and nine who worked seven days a week, 65 to 75 hours. Our conversation immediately turned kinetic. Someone jumped in to say: "Child labor is the worst kind of unfair competition. No wonder the U.S. is in trouble." Someone else argued that the real unfairness was to the children and women themselves: "Doesn't the Bangladesh manufacturer understand that they are human beings, blessed with God-given dignity?"

The returnee from Bangladesh, however, was not finished. Senser broke in: "What

> **DO PARISH-BASED PEACE**
> and justice committees spend too little time equipping fellow parishioners for their crucial work in the world?

do you want first, the good news or the bad news? The good news is that no U.S. capital is invested in these garment factories. But the bad news is that two of our country's largest retailers import these garments."

Pope John Paul II, the author of *Centesimus Annus*, was not present at our gathering. But were he there, I am sure he would immediately have asked: What can be done about such exploitation? Who can end this injustice? How soon?

Centesimus Annus and the rest of the encyclical tradition is more than Catholic social *thought*. Its purpose is to turn ideas into action, to make a lively connection between faith and work, to set forces in motion, which will bring about change, realize justice. The context for the encyclical tradition is not the classroom or the Sunday congregation. It is the marketplace. The workplace. The neighborhood. The global economy. Deeds speak louder than words.

The encyclical tradition—from 1891 to today—carries a daunting set of core imperatives for leaders of business, government, the labor movement, and education. Social policy, first. Social thought, second.

But in the U.S. church has social action been overshadowed by the emphasis on Catholic social teaching? Do parish-based peace and justice committees spend too much time navel gazing and too little time equipping fellow parishioners for their crucial work in the world?

A centerpiece of the encyclical tradition is the principle of subsidiary. Yet the ironic weakness of the Catholic social tradition, especially its U.S. expression, is the neglect of an urban agenda for the 21st century. In its preoccupation with Catholic social *thought*, this tradition has largely ignored the malfunctioning of our municipal institutions, city agencies such as public school systems, community colleges and public housing authorities. These institutions are no longer mainstreaming the cities' poor as they once did. In graduate schools of public policy, students are taught how to make good policies and how to shun making bad ones. But seldom do we teach students how to undo good urban policies gone bad….

The encyclical tradition, especially John Paul II's contributions, is out to spark questions, to kindle soul-searching. What kind of questions?

In a recent article Mary Jo Bane and David Ellwood from the John Kennedy School of Government ask, "Is American business working for the poor?" They discern a direct link between corporate performance and poverty, insisting that companies cannot create the work force of the future with the social policies of the past. Are they correct?

In his farewell address, Harvard University President Derek Bok focused on "The Social Responsibilities of American Universities," and opened with the question: "Is it enough for Harvard to attract the brightest students if we do not excel in making them caring, active, enlightened citizens and civic leaders?" Bok continued: "In asking this question I do not mean in any way to suggest that we should press upon students any particular social policy or economic doctrine…. But neither should we accept the view, so prevalent in our society, that it is somehow politically correct to tolerate our domestic problems and stand by when there is so much work to be done to revitalize our nation."

Judaism, Islam and Christianity inevitably are iconoclastic religions, striving to tumble false gods in order to turn our attention to important questions like these: Is consumerism a counterfeit god? Is it the other side of the coin of Karl Marx's materialism?

Thomas Johnson, former president of Manufacturer's Hanover Trust, underlines the recurring need to debunk an enshrined ideology. In doing so, he poses a question: "John Paul II clearly endorses free enterprise.... But the Pope also expresses grave misgivings over 'the many human needs that find no place on the market.' He writes of wrenching poverty juxtaposed with what he calls 'an idolatry of the markets.' The nub of the Pope's concerns can be expressed in a simple question: How can we address the unmet needs of people in a market economy without damaging the market's special genius for stimulating initiative and productivity?"

> HOW CAN WE ADDRESS
> the unmet needs of people in a market economy without damaging the market's special genius for stimulating initiative and productivity?

The gospel of St. Matthew recounts the parable about a master who gave each of his servants, according to their abilities, a different number of talents. The parable's message is similar to the purpose of John Paul II's encyclical *Centesimus Annus*. It is not so much about a more equitable distribution of talents, but about what the servants had done with them. It is about their stewardship. An encyclical is not an academic treatise to be passed on by one generation of professors to the next. The encyclical tradition always prompts questions: What did we do with our talents? Did we mothball them? Or did we use our talents to "let justice roll down like mighty water and righteousness as an ever flowing stream?"

MARY IRENE ZOTTI

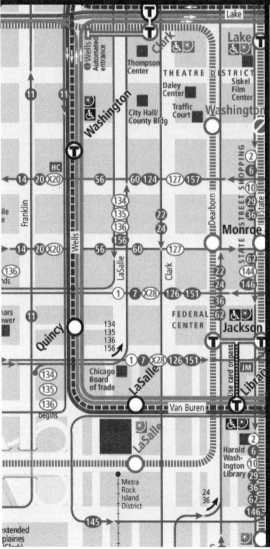

1921 -

Back in the mid-1940s, Monsignor John Hayes, a good friend of the great Monsignor Reynold Hillenbrand, recommended one of his high school students, Mary Irene Zotti, for a Catholic Action program. Hayes and Hillenbrand were so impressed with Zotti that they arranged for her to visit Europe and study the origins of the "specialized Catholic Action movements."

Zotti earned degrees from Loyola University and Chicago State University (called Chicago Teachers College back then). She then spent 22 years in Chicago public schools as a guidance counselor and librarian, occasionally taking a turn in the classroom. She and her husband, Ray, celebrated their golden wedding anniversary at the turn of the new century. They raised six children and are grandparents to 18 grandchildren.

I see Zotti at every gathering of the Church, Chicago-style tribe. First it was at conferences and at anniversary or retirement banquets. Now it is more often at funerals, most recently that of her friend and fellow Young Christian Worker, Mary Buckley, one of the co-founders of ACTA Publications.

In the following essay, taken from her book, *Time of Awakening: The Young Christian Worker Story in the United States, 1938-1970* (Loyola University Press, 1991), Zotti chronicles the rise and fall of the Young Christian Worker movement in Chicago and elsewhere. Like the Young Christian Students and the Christian Family Movement, YCW was part of "the lay apostolate" or "specialized Catholic Action." (The term *Catholic Action* is capitalized when used to refer to these recognized lay movements, because the terms *Catholic Action* and *lay apostolate* once had a precise meaning and suggested a very specific model of how the church is positioned in the world.) Catholic Action was part of the mix at Vatican II, but other, perhaps better, models of social justice emerged from the Council. Catholic Action, more or less, presumed a hierarchical model of the church that gave way to a more horizontal or circular model at and after the Council. Thus the Vatican II documents contain a tension between an older style of lay involvement and a less defined, emerging style. The tension was the topic for many discussions and a few arguments among the Chicago leaders in the years just before and after Vatican II. Zotti's study of the rise and fall of YCW is extremely significant in this context.

Basically, Catholic Action or the lay apostolate was conceived, as expressed by Pope Pius XI in 1931, as "participation of the laity in the apostolate of the hierarchy." It was seen as a way of encouraging the laity to bring the gospel to the modern, pluralistic world where the church was one actor among many. It was a world where Church officials could no longer regularly consort with monarchs, local lords or town rulers. The church, for the better, had to return to its earliest model—where laypeople were the ministers or apostles in daily circumstances.

Additionally, the lay apostolate movement, as shaped by Cardinal Joseph Cardijn of Belgium beginning in the late 1920s, offered young working people in Europe's industrial centers sound intellectual and moral foundation, as an alternative to the Communist and Socialist movements. Cardijn and other chaplains formed small groups of miners, dock workers, factory hands, secretaries and more. In a process described here by Zotti, the small groups studied their faith and pledged to apply it in daily life.

Vatican II stressed baptism, not priestly ordination, as the foundation for the church's mission in and to the world. At first this seemed to fit with the Catholic Action model, but it really signaled a shift. The post-Vatican II laity are no longer to be seen as merely participating in the ministry of the clergy and hierarchy but as having a vocation of their own in the workplace, family life and community affairs. The lay faithful "seek the kingdom of God by engaging in temporal affairs and directing them according to God's will," says Vatican II's *Dogmatic Constitution on the Church.* "They live in the world. That is, they are engaged in each and every work and business of the earth and in the ordinary circumstances of family life…. [The laity] contribute to the sanctification of the world, as from within like leaven, by fulfilling their ordinary duties."

> THE POST VATICAN II LAITY are no longer to be seen as merely participating in the ministry of the clergy and hierarchy but as having a vocation of their own in the workplace, family life and community affairs.

The term *lay apostolate* has fallen into disuse today. At the same time, there is no consensus on what term to use for the apostolic activity Christians perform in the world today. Some Protestants speak of "ministry in daily life," while some Catholics and others refer to "the spirituality of work" or "the mission to transform the world." What is common to pre-Vatican II Catholic Action and the new theology is the idea of laypeople connecting their faith with their real daily life. The ramifications of this idea are still playing out, and there is much gold to be mined in the history of the Church, Chicago-style.

HISTORY OF THE YOUNG CHRISTIAN WORKERS
Mary Irene Zotti

T hough our activities in the early Catholic Action cells were small and seemingly inconsequential, they marked a new departure for the American church. They represented a positive first step in the development of thinking, acting laity. Key to this development was the involvement of priests who would take the work of lay people seriously and encourage their action....

One of a handful of forward-looking priests in the 1930s, Monsignor Reynold Hillenbrand combined his natural talents, his love of the Church, and his sensitivity to human need to become a leading figure in the development of new answers to an old question: how to spread the teachings of Christ in the world. He recognized that the world itself was the creation of God and the proper setting in which Christians should work out their eternal destiny....

When he was appointed as rector of St. Mary of the Lake Seminary in 1936, Cardinal George Mundelein introduced him to the seminarians with the words, "I've brought you a man with imagination."

> HILLENBRAND SAW ACTIVE participation of the laity in the liturgical worship of the church and the advocacy of labor unions for a living wage as two sides of the same coin: human beings must be fed in soul and body.

Poet and preacher and lover of God, a man of deep insight and strong will, Hillenbrand put his visionary stamp on the seminary during eight exciting years. The seminarians were exposed to new understandings about liturgical worship and social action. Hillenbrand saw active participation of the laity in the liturgical worship of the church and the advocacy of labor unions for a living wage as two sides of the same coin: human beings must be fed in soul and body....

The strength and fortitude of this devoted man is probably the prime reason that Chicago became a national center of the Catholic Action movement....

Hillenbrand was concerned about the working man who had to support a family. He and his friend Monsignor John Hayes were strong supporters of union causes and programs like the Catholic Worker, which sought to alleviate the basic needs of workers suffering the effects of social injustice. Father Gerry Weber recalls Hayes handing out copies of Dorothy Day's *Catholic Worker* in his algebra class at Quigley Preparatory Seminary in 1933....

The easiest part of this new lay movement for people to understand was the small group base. The graphic picture of the church as the Mystical Body of Christ made the concept of the cell very clear. Moreover, the support of the small group was invaluable when members attempted to influence others....

A large loose-leaf binder of minutes kept by the secretary of one Chicago working girls' cell from July 1939 to December 1940 reveals a fairly typical story....

Each week the group used the Sunday Gospel for their New Testament discussion and drew a conclusion applied to the work of Catholic Action. For example, when the Gospel of Matthew 22: 35-46 cited Christ's answer to the Pharisees about the great commandment of love of God and its corollary about love of neighbor, the conclusion drawn [by the girls] was, "As Christ was able to answer the Pharisees in such a way that they could find no fault or reason for contention, so we should try to grow in knowledge of the faith so we too could find satisfactory answers." This conclusion reveals the mindset of the members. A group supposedly involved in apostolic action apparently missed the key idea in the passage about love of one's neighbor....

By the time the group had been meeting a year several new members had been added and the girls had learned a lot of answers to what today might be called trivia questions. Details about religious belief and observance were of primary concern. The group by now consisted of a department store cashier, two telephone operators, a bank page girl, one general office worker, and one girl who was unemployed.

On June 28, 1940, members of the group attended the meeting of lay leaders at Holy Name Cathedral where Father Louis Putz, CSC stressed the idea of service as a way of influencing others. It evidently sank in, for in the minutes of August 21, 1940, acts of service were reported for the first time. A few weeks later, moreover, one member went out of her way to sit next to a black person on a bus, even though there were plenty of empty seats. This incident indicated the beginning of a new awareness toward minorities. In the inquiry section of the meetings, members began to report on "doing Catholic Action," and "influencing people with whom we come in contact." In October 1940, one member came to the conclusion that "we are influenced by others around us more than we realize."

In the fall of 1940, the Chicago chaplains met with chaplains from throughout the country and agreed to a common meeting plan. They had been reading through reports from the cells and were appalled to find that many groups were not using the inquiry method at all. Cell members did not know what to look for and did not ask probing questions that would bring out the facts. It was only after a year that the girls in the group just described began to look at what people were doing instead of answering their questions about religion....

[In 1951] Father Edward Mitchinson, national chaplain of the English YCW, wrote an article, ["The Doctrine of Working"] that became a standard treatise for the English-speaking [Catholic Action] movements.

> YOUR MISSION IS NOT just with rod and line, not just with the net, but that it is of changing the water in which the fish must live.

In the YCW, we are vitally concerned not only with the redemption of persons but with the redemption of things, of surroundings, of institutions. We have the mission of "restoring things in Christ." We know that the young workers will be saved or damned eternally in and through the environment in which they live. You know so well that your mission is not just with rod and line, not just with the net, but that it is of changing the water in which the fish must live. We must realize that the world of matter must be transformed and Christianized, not only as a means of aiding the redemption of men but in order that created nature may present a true pattern of glory to God. In Christ "all things came into being, and without Him came nothing that has come to be." (1 John 3) Through sin came disorder into the world. Through redemption continued in the apostolate, all things, the whole order of nature, must be restored in Christ.

Monsignor Hillenbrand emphasized this idea at the 1953 Study Week:

> We are dedicated to an institutional apostolate. We are not out just to change individuals; we're out to change things, the things which endure when the people change, when the people move on, when people die. We want laws which will help people who come after. We want labor unions to stay in a plant after we are gone....
>
> On the other side, we also have to change people and give them the idea of justice. You have to give them the idea of charity, but charity without justice is a complete fraud.... I don't want your charity. You are not giving me justice [as a present].... I want the basic things due me as a human being.

MIDDLE-CLASS AFFLUENCE, increased social and occupational mobility among young people, the lack of positive support from the hierarchy, the changes in societal values, the youth rebellion against authority—all these contributed to the demise of the Young Christian Workers as an organized movement in the United States.

In spite of such encouraging developments, problems at the local level were beginning to surface. Membership in the movement was not growing as might have been expected. From a peak somewhat over 3,000 at the end of the 1950s, it dropped to 2,500 in the early 1960s. Moreover, rapid turnover in the membership was becoming apparent. For every ten new sections, ten or 12 were folding. As the United States shifted from an industrial economy to a service economy and more young people opted for higher education, it was hard to attract new members who would or could stay in a section the recommended three years. Moreover, the average marrying age by the late 1950s reached an all-time low. This seriously reduced the number of available singe young workers....

The early 1960s were paradoxical for the Young Christian Workers. On the one hand, they were encouraged by the words of Pope John XXIII who promoted the See, Judge, Act method in his 1962 encyclical and the acceptance of the specialized movements by the National Catholic Welfare Conference. On the other hand, the movement was not expanding. There seemed to be two main reasons: (1) The rigid educational program [of YCW] was out of touch with the real needs of young people, and (2) affluent young Americans didn't think of themselves as workers.

Was the movement failing because it was becoming irrelevant? This is a question the YCW/YCM leaders of the early 1960s did not ask, in fact could not ask, so totally committed were they to the need for a lay apostolate among young workers....

The decline in YCW membership in the early years of the 1960s had been largely a result of complacency, but as the decade wore on, disenchantment with the Church became the dominant factor. Loss of membership was most pronounced in the Midwest. Many of the remaining active sections were in Hispanic neighborhoods on the East and West coasts....

Hillenbrand's unlimited faith in the old ways was reinforced by the encouraging words of John XXIII and the decrees of the Vatican Council. Hillenbrand did not seem to realize that a rapidly changing world might need new solutions and he continued to be the guru of the movement's leadership....

There are no sections [of YCW] in Chicago after 1968....

Middle-class affluence, increased social and occupational mobility among young people, the lack of positive support from the hierarchy, the changes in societal values, the youth rebellion against authority—all these contributed to the demise of the Young Christian Workers as an organized movement in the United States. Internal problems related to the quality of leadership in the last decade and the lack of a full-time chaplain were the other factors that weakened the movement. In the end its apostolic view of "A new youth for a new world" became irrelevant. Fast-moving changes in the world had outstripped its progressive goals. It no longer fit the times....

Because the times and the culture changed drastically in the 1960s, the kind of moral and social reform which motivated the Young Christian Workers in earlier decades no longer seemed to meet the needs of the younger generation. It was supplanted by single issue movements concerned with civil rights, ecology, women's rights, peace, and so on. The Young Christian Workers had anticipated many of the new movements in their action programs, especially the civil rights movement.

The changes in the church precipitated by the Second Vatican Council also played a role in the demise of the apostolic movements throughout the world. Pluralism as affirmed in John XXIII's encyclical *Pacem in Terris* allowed for widely varying opinions as to the way the presence of the church should be manifested. The creative responsibility of the lay person in the modern world, as developed in [Vatican II's *Pastoral Constitution on the Church in the Modern World*] *Gaudium et Spes*, seemed clear enough, but rapid and complex changes in society made specific directions uncertain. No longer did the church claim to have all the answers for society. Evangelism and ecumenism seemed a contradiction....

What did seem significant to the American Young Christian Workers was the announcement [at about the time of Vatican II] that the specialized Catholic Action movements in the United States, including YCW, YCS, and CFM were to become part of the official Church structure under the umbrella of the National Catholic Welfare Conference, [later called the U.S. Catholic Conference of Bishops]. This represented quite a turnabout. Years earlier, the YCW leaders had decided not to identify their organization as official Catholic Action which was under the control of the hierarchy, so that they could remain free to go their own way.

[Ironically,] changes in the church precipitated by Vatican II played a role in the demise of the apostolic movements.... [After Vatican II] the pastoral concern of the [Church headquarters in Washington, in diocesan Chanceries and elsewhere] seemed to turn in on itself. The certainty of a worldly vision which characterized the pre-Vatican II church [at least in Catholic Action movements] was gone. There was nothing to replace it.

NATIONAL CENTER
FOR THE LAITY

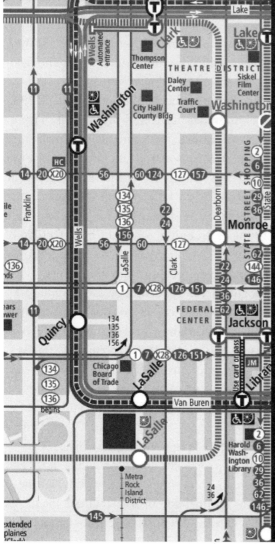

1978 -

One day in the middle 1970s Ed Marciniak, whose office was within binocular distance of the Archdiocesan Chancery Office, saw an oddity across the street: the Chicago Priests' Senate formed a "committee on the laity." Marciniak thought it strange that only priests were on the committee. Fortunately, so too did Marciniak's close friend and the committee chair, Monsignor Dan Cantwell.

Cantwell quickly expanded the group to include bankers, journalists, homemakers, union officials, lawyers, women religious, students and others.

It was Advent 1977 when those 47 prominent Chicago Catholics issued *A Chicago Declaration of Christian Concern* (reprinted below).

The *Chicago Declaration* hit a nerve. Conferences, radio programs, and scores of articles debated its implications. Nearly two million copies were eventually distributed.

The *Chicago Declaration* generated so much mail that a secretariat quickly became necessary. That office, first housed at Mundelein College, was called the National Center for the Laity.

As the months went by the NCL formed a board of directors, filed for separate incorporation, began publishing an acclaimed newsletter titled *INITIATIVES*, held conferences and retreats, and developed a network of individuals and institutions that share the concern voiced in the 1977 *Chicago Declaration*.

I came upon the NCL as a graduate student at Mundelein College in 1980. To be honest, the NCL was dormant within two years of its origin. Only a handful of people was holding the fort: Larry Ragan, Larry Suffredin, Bill Spielberger, Stephanie Certain, Russ Barta, and Cantwell and Marciniak. But because it was a vessel for the best of the Chicago-style and a carrier of the Vatican II vision, I wanted to revive the NCL (or, if necessary, start a comparable organization). In any case, Chicago—I judged—needed a transfusion. Thus I asked my high school friends, Greg Pierce at that time of Brooklyn, NY, and Chuck DiSalvo of Morgantown, WV, to help. Pierce became NCL president and eventually moved to Chicago, throwing a substantial portion of his energy into the cause. DiSalvo, doing long distance legal service, obtained independent legal incorporation for NCL and developed a business plan. Mary Beth Dunne of Albany, NY, a judge and homemaker who attended the NCL founding convention in 1978, was brought back into our circle. Other out-of-town talent was recruited to the NCL board: people like Gerry Shea, a welfare rights advocate and union leader from Washington, DC, Peggy Steinfels, a Chicago native who was editing *Commonweal* magazine in New York City, Kathy Hidy, a homemaker, teacher and lawyer in Cincinnati, OH, Rose Hart, a letter carrier in West Virginia, and Clyde Evans, a health care expert from Boston, MA. Then we found several new Chicago leaders, people who came of age *after* Vatican II: people like Tom Donnelly, a judge and law professor, Patty Dondanville Berman, a corporate attorney, Judy Valente, a TV and radio journalist, Janet Olson, a grammar school teacher and homemaker, Frosty Pipal, a mediator and lawyer, and a few others who were contemporaries of the people in this book, including Phil Moore, John Hazard, Vaile Scott and Bruce Rattenbury.

The NCL now has a Chicago-based board and a national advisory group. There are about 80 churches, Newman centers and organizations in a fledgling NCL network. There are 5,000 readers of the NCL newsletter *INITIATIVES* in the U.S., Canada and seven other countries.

As it approached its 25th anniversary, the NCL assessed the state of the question by convening several regional dinners in places like Joliet, DeKalb, Toledo, Morgantown, Hoboken, Cincinnati, New York and Corvallis. Then a major conference was held in Chicago. Out of that process came the second document in this chapter, *Nine Principles for Lay Initiative*.

A CHICAGO DECLARATION
OF CHRISTIAN CONCERN
by the National Center for the Laity

T he signers of this *Declaration* are members of the Catholic community in Chicago.

For decades, the church in Chicago nurtured a compelling vision of lay Christians in society. The vision was eventually accepted and celebrated by the Second Vatican Council. That same vision produced national movements and networks which generated a dynamic lay leadership. It attracted priests and religious who saw their ministry as arousing the laity to the pursuit of justice and freedom; who served the laity without manipulating them.

Shall we passively accept that period of history as completely over, and with it the vision that proved to be so creative? While many in the Church exhaust their energies arguing internal issues, albeit important

> THE LAITY WHO SPEND most of their time and energy in the professional and occupational world appear to have been deserted.

ones, such as the ordination of women and a married clergy, the laity who spend most of their time and energy in the professional and occupational world appear to have been deserted.

"Without a vision the people shall perish." Who now sustains lay persons as they meet the daily challenges of their job and profession—the arena in which questions of justice and peace are really located? Where are the movements and organizations supporting the young toward a Christian maturity? Where are the priests [and other Church professionals] sufficiently self-assured in their own identity and faith that they can devote themselves to energizing leaders committed to reforming the structures of society?

We wait impatiently for a new prophecy, a new word that can once again stir people to see the grandeur of the Christian vision for society and move priests [and other Church professionals] to galvanize people in their secular-religious role.

We think that this new prophecy should retrieve, at least in part, the best insights of Vatican II. It was Vatican II that broadened our understanding of the church. It rejected the notion that church is to be identified exclusively with hierarchical roles—such as bishop and priest. The church is as present to the world in the ordinary roles of Christians as it is in the ecclesiastical roles of bishop and priest, though the styles of each differ.

Vatican II identified hopes for social justice and world peace with the church's saving mission. The salvation of the world is no longer to be construed as applying only to individual persons but embraces all the institutions of society. The church is present to the world in the striving of the laity to transform the world of political, economic and social institutions. The clergy [and other Church professionals] minister so that the laity will exercise their family, neighborly and occupational roles mindful of their Christian responsibility. The thrust of Vatican II is unmistakable:

> What specifically characterizes the laity is their secular nature. It is true that those in holy orders can at times be engaged in secular activities, and even have a secular profession. But they are, by reason of their particular vocation, especially and professedly ordained to the sacred ministry. Similarly, by their state in life, religious give splendid and striking testimony that the world cannot be transformed and offered to God without the spirit of the beatitudes. But the laity, by their special vocation, seek the kingdom of God by engaging in temporal affairs and by ordering them according to the plan of God. They live in the world, that is, in each and in all of the secular professions and occupations. They live in the ordinary circumstances of family and social life, from which the very web of their existence is woven. Today they are called by God, that by exercising their proper function, and led by the spirit of the Gospel, they may work for the sanctification of the world from within as a leaven. In this way they may make Christ known to others, especially by the testimony of a life resplendent in faith, hope and charity. Therefore, since they are tightly bound up in all types of temporal affairs, it is their special task to order and to throw light upon

those affairs in such a way that they may be made and grow according to Christ to the praise of the creator and redeemer. (*Dogmatic Constitution on the Church*, #31)

Although the teaching of Vatican II on the ministry of the laity is forceful and represents one of the Council's most notable achievements, in recent years it seems to have all but vanished from the consciousness and agendas of many sectors within the church.

It is our experience that a wholesome and significant movement within the church—the involvement of lay people in many Church ministries—has led to a devaluation of the unique ministry of lay women and men. The tendency has been to see lay ministry as involvement in some Church related activity, e.g. religious education, pastoral care for the sick and elderly, or readers in church on Sunday. Thus lay ministry is seen as participation in work traditionally assigned to priests or religious.

We recognize the new opportunities opened up to men to become permanent deacons, but believe that in the long run such programs will be a disaster if they create the impression that only in such fashion do the laity mainly participate in the

> A WHOLESOME AND significant movement within the church—the involvement of lay people in many Church ministries—has led to a devaluation of the unique ministry of lay women and men.

mission of the church. We note that our misgivings are shared by the Apostolic Delegate to the U.S., Archbishop Jean Jadot, who commented recently: "I believe in the laity. And the laity as laity. I was very, very impressed, I must say, by my experiences in Africa and my closeness and friendliness with some African bishops who don't want to hear about a permanent diaconate. They say it will kill the laity in the church. It will kill the laity in the church because it will reinforce the conviction already existing that to work for the church you must be ordained."

Our own reaction to the 1976 Detroit Call To Action conference reflects a similar ambivalence. Without a doubt, it was historic, precedent-setting in its conception, in its consultative process, in helping all levels of the church listen to each other and in facing challenges to growth affecting the inner life of the church. But devoting, as it did, so much of its time to the internal affairs of the Church, the conference did not sufficiently illuminate the broader mission of the church to the world and the indispensable role of lay Christians in carrying out that mission.

During the last decade especially, many priests [and other Church profession-als] have acted as if the primary responsibility in the church for uprooting injus-tice, ending wars and defending human rights rested with them. As a result they bypassed the laity to pursue social causes on their own rather than enabling lay Christians to shoulder their own responsibility. These priests and religious have sought to impose their own agendas for the world upon the laity. Indeed, if in the past the Church has suffered from a clericalism on the right, it may now face the threat of a revived clericalism—on the left.

We also note with concern the steady depreciation, during the past decade, of the ordinary social roles through which the laity serve and act upon the world. The impression is often created that one can work for justice and peace only by stepping outside of these ordinary roles as a business person, as a mayor, as a factory worker, as a professional in the State Department, or as an active union member and thus that one can change the system only as an outsider to the society and the system.

> THE IMPRESSION IS OFTEN created that one can work for justice and peace only by stepping outside of these ordinary roles and thus that one can change the system only as an outsider to the society and the system.

Such ideas clearly depart from the mainstream of Catholic social thought which regards the advance of social justice as essentially the service performed within one's professional and occupational milieu. The almost exclusive preoc-cupation with the role of the outsider as the model for social action can only dis-tract the laity from the apostolic potential that lies at the core of their professional and occupational lives.

Although we do not hold them up as models adequate to present-day needs, we do note with regret the decline and, too often, the demise of those organizations and networks of the recent past whose task it was to inspire and support Christians in their vocation to the world through their professional and occupational lives. We have in mind such organizations as the National Catholic Social Action Conference, the National Conference of Christian Employers and Managers, the Association of Catholic Trade Unionists, the National Council of Catholic Nurses, Young Christian Students, Young Christian Workers, and the Catholic Council on Working Life.

Although concerns for justice and peace are now built into Church bureaucracy more so than when such organizations flourished, there is no evidence that such bureaucratization has led to further involvement of lay Christians. As a matter of fact, the disappearance of organizations like the above, and our failure to replace them, may have resulted in the loss of a generation of Catholic leadership.

As various secular ideologies—including communism, socialism and liberalism—each in turn fail to live up to their promise to transform radically the human condition, some Christians seek to convert religion and the Gospel itself into another political ideology. Although we also yearn for a new heaven and a new earth, we insist that the Gospel of Jesus Christ by itself reveals no political or economic program to bring this about. Direct appeals to the Gospel in order to justify specific solutions to social problems, whether domestic or international, are really a betrayal of the Gospel. The Good News calling for peace, justice and freedom needs to be mediated through the prism of experience, political wisdom and technical expertise. Christian social thought is a sophisticated body of social wisdom which attempts such mediation, supplying the middle ground between the Gospel on the one hand and the concrete decisions which Christians make on their own responsibility in their everyday life.

In conclusion, we address these words of hope and of deep concern to the members of the church throughout the nation as well as to members of the church in Chicago. We invite them to associate themselves with this *Declaration*. We prayerfully anticipate that our words and theirs will prompt a re-examination of present tendencies in the church and that out of such a re-examination will emerge a new sense of direction, a new agenda.

In the last analysis, the church speaks to and acts upon the world through her laity. Without a dynamic laity conscious of its personal ministry to the world, the church, in effect, does not speak or act. No amount of social action by priests and religious can ever be an adequate substitute for enhancing lay responsibility. The absence of lay initiative can only take us down the road to clericalism. We are deeply concerned that so little energy is devoted to encouraging and arousing lay responsibility for the world. The church must constantly be reformed, but we fear that the almost obsessive preoccupation with the Church's structures and processes has diverted attention from the essential question: reform for what purpose? It would be one of the great ironies of history if the era of Vatican II which opened the windows of the church to the world were to close with a church turned in upon itself.

Third Sunday of the Coming of the Lord, 1977
Original Signers of the *Chicago Declaration* and their titles in 1977:

Russell Barta, Professor of Sociology, Mundelein College
Albert J. Belanger, Alliance of Catholic Laity
Cecelia Brocken, Associate Dean, College of Health Sciences, Rush University
Martin J. Burns, Attorney
Sr. M. Josetta Butler, RSM, Past President, St. Xavier College
Morris Bohannon, Service Analysis Officer, U.S. Postal Service
Monsignor Daniel M. Cantwell, Pastor, St. Clotilde Parish
Father Alcuin Coyle, OFM, President, Catholic Theological Union
Patty Crowley, Co-Founder of the Christian Family Movement
Sr. Agnes Cunningham, SSCM, President, Catholic Theological Society
    of America
Dorothy A. Drain, Religion Editor, Chicago Defender
Susan Durburg, Psychiatric Nursing Consultant, Evanston Hospital
Father James Finno, Associate Pastor, St. Mary Parish, Evanston
Father John E. Flavin, President, Presbyterial Senate of the Archdiocese
    of Chicago
Father Vincent Giese, Our Lady of Perpetual Help Church
Father Raymond E. Goedert. Pastor, St. Barnabas Parish
Patrick E. Gorman, Chairman of the Board, Amalgamated Meat Cutters
    and Butchers

Father Robert F. Harvanek, SJ, Professor of Philosophy, Loyola University

Sr. Carol Frances Jegen, BVM, Professor of Religious Studies, Mundelein College

Bishop King, Assistant to Superintendent for Minority Groups,
    Archdiocesan Schools

Thaddeus L. Kowalski, President, Polish American Congress, Illinois Division

George Leighton, Judge, United States District Court, Northern District
    of Illinois

Franklin McMahon, Artist-Reporter

Irene Leahy McMahon, Writer-Homemaker

Ed Marciniak, President, Institute of Urban Life; Chair, Center for Urban
    Ethnic Affairs

Eugene P. Moats, President, Local 25, Service Employees International Union

Samuel W. Nolan, Deputy Superintendent, Chicago Police Department

Edward J. Noonan, Architect; President of Chicago Associates

Robert Olmstead, Reporter

Father John Pawlikowski, OSM, Associate Professor, Catholic Theological Union

Faustin A. Pipal, Chairman of the Board, St. Paul Federal Savings & Loan

Jorge Prieto, MD, Chairman, Department of Family Medicine,
    Cook County Hospital

Luz-Maria Prieto, Director, Mujeres Latinas en Accion

Lawrence Ragan, Editor, The Ragan Report

Bruce Rattenbury, Director of Public Relations, Rush-Presbyterian
    St. Luke Medical

Jolyn H. Robichaux, President, Baldwin Ice Cream Co.

Edmund J. Rooney, Reporter, Chicago daily News

Mary Schiltz, Project Associate, Institute of Urban Life

Don Servatius, President, Local 165, International Brotherhood of
    Electrical Workers

Father John Shea, Instructor in Systematic Theology, St. Mary of the
    Lake Seminary

Father Carroll Stuhmueller, CP, President-elect, Catholic Biblical
    Association of America

Lawrence J. Suffredin, Attorney

William H. Tate, Chairman of the Board, CCT Press, Ltd.
Dan Tucker, Member of the Editorial Board, Chicago Tribune
Father Thomas Ventura, Chairman, Association of Chicago Priests
Father John J. Wall, Instructor in Theology, Niles College, Loyola University
Anne Zimmerman, Executive Administrator, Illinois Nurses' Association

NINE PRINCIPLES FOR LAY INITIATIVE
by the National Center for the Laity

PRINCIPLE #1: ENCOUNTERING GOD

People are constantly sought out and confronted by God in the midst of life's hustle and bustle—not away from it. Correspondingly, it is a religious duty for Christians to attend to the signs of God's presence in everyday life, for—in the words of Vatican II—"nothing genuinely human fails to raise an echo in the hearts of the followers of Christ."

IMPLICATIONS:

- All preaching, catechesis, social action ministry, worship, acts of citizenship, work, leisure and neighborliness must take into account the sacred potential in what appears to be mundane human experience. For embedded in the ordinary lies the extraordinary, the miraculous, the saving, and the holy. Pastoral practice must come to recognize that the exchange of love between God and God's people is mediated through our grace-filled, created world—just as it is through the Sunday Eucharist.

- Contemplation is indeed a prerequisite for thoughtful action. Lay spirituality, however, eventually turns toward the world. Spiritual direction or spiritual programs that tend to steer people away from the world are not helpful to most Christians because the path of salvation and the life of the church courses through the experience of parents, students, workers, neighbors, friends and spouses.

- The truth is that God so loved the world that God became a baby in a trough, a carpenter, a common criminal on a cross, a human being—a coworker in an office, a neighbor, a machinist, a customer, a middle-manager, a nurse, an accountant, a spouse. Through the redemptive love of Christ we are called to make our lives a little sacrament...raised up, broken and blessed... bread of and for the people we meet on the job, around the home and in the neighborhood.

PRINCIPLE #2: ROLE OF THE LAITY

The best apostles in a given situation are usually those Christians closest to the situation. Their proper and important roles should be respected, their gifts acknowledged and their competency cultivated and utilized.

IMPLICATIONS:

- The initiative to gather with like-minded Christians and to transform the world should be taken up without hesitation by each baptized person. Christian women and men should not wait for programs emanating from a rectory or diocesan agency in order to shoulder their responsibility in the world. Today's laity gladly cooperate with priests, religious and other Church employees who support and challenge them to live their faith in the home, the neighborhood and the marketplace.

- The potential of the laity is best used when they are challenged and supported to live the gospel in their everyday lives. Too much attention to lay ministry inside the Church has, it seems, preempted attention to the laity's vocation in the world. It is a blessing to the church that so many lay people are acquiring ministerial degrees and are volunteering for pastoral ministries. This burst of lay ministry is not, however, to be understood as dependent upon a relative shortage of the ordained nor is it to be seen by anyone as superior to ordinary lay activity in the world nor should it come at the expense of the laity's vocation in the world.

PRINCIPLE #3: CONCERTED ACTION

Whenever possible, lay initiative should be ecumenical and interfaith.

IMPLICATION:

Catholic parishes and movements should guide and support their own members while at the same time encouraging those members to join with their neighbors, coworkers and colleagues to humanize social, political and cultural institutions.

PRINCIPLE #4: WISDOM FROM NORTH AMERICA

Positive spiritual impulses have always moved across and through the North American continent.

IMPLICATIONS:

- The North American experience with its history of immigration, its praxis of mediating institutions, its respect for diversity within unity, its freedom of religious expression, and its arts of negotiation and conflict resolution is consistent with Catholic social teaching and, as such, affords an opportunity for reflection in order to deepen Christian wisdom. Preaching, catechesis, and church programs can develop lessons from the strengths of North American culture.

- At the same time, North American culture tends to be too individualistic, materialistic and relativistic. Wherever the culture falls short of the City of God, Christians have a duty to raise human consciousness and direct the culture toward the common good.

- Theology developed in Germany, France, England, Poland, Latin America and elsewhere is a blessing to the universal church. But the universal church could greatly benefit from more reflection on the North American experience. In particular, North American Catholic spirituality (a la Orestes Brownson, Cesar Chavez, Dorothy Day, Catherine de Hueck Doherty, Father Isaac Hecker, Archbishop John Ireland, Ed Marciniak and others) needs to be reclaimed.

PRINCIPLE #5: SOCIAL CHANGE

A critical virtue for the laity is social justice. The intended outcome of social justice is a better policy or an improved institution. To practice social justice requires an organized initiative. Christians do not normally effect change as lone rangers.

IMPLICATIONS:

- The laity need forums in which they can learn more about social virtues and their application to daily life on the job, around the home and in the neighborhood. In particular, people need more tools for understanding how they are often manipulated by culture and institutions. Likewise, people need tools for countering the mediocre and the evil in their own institutions.

- People who take collective action on the job, in their professions or in their communities need support and deserve respect from the whole church.

- The urge for inner peace is a healthy one. However, a genuine Catholic lay spirituality does not neglect the virtue of social justice, the exercise of which may be emotionally disturbing. Collective inaction cannot be excused. It is an error to wait until each person has inner peace and integrity before one gets involved. People who, for example, marched in Selma in the cause of civil rights did not wait to change all their imperfections. In part, their souls were changed simply by marching.

PRINCIPLE #6: HOLINESS OF WORK

Work is participation in God's on-going creation and participation in Christ's redemption. Good work is how women and men, individually and collectively, offer their best to the earthly city and to the City of God. Work itself is capable of contributing to the spiritual life.

IMPLICATIONS:

- Major ethical issues abound in the everyday world of work. Inhumane working conditions, unethical practices and unresponsive social structures blemish the plan of God. There is, however, a Christian optimism about what is developing in technology, science, industry, construction, commerce, the arts and other areas of human endeavor. There is a strong affinity between openness to the future and Christian hope.

- Courses, publications and associations dedicated to business, legal or medical ethics are needed. More crucial still are forums which help the laity grapple—not simply with ethics—but, in the words of Vatican II, with "the meaning of all this feverish activity."

PRINCIPLE #7: BLESSING THE ORDINARY

People do God's will in their jobs, in their families and in neighborhoods when they act with love, justice, integrity and care. This should be recognized and celebrated by the whole church.

IMPLICATIONS:

- When moralizers, in broad strokes, dismiss or condemn the legal profession, electoral politics, or business, conscientious lay people are offended. It's easy for outsiders to the system to feel a sense of superiority by echoing moral slogans. Christian insiders, on the other hand, are not always certain they are right, but they are seasoned enough in the real world to resist simplicities.

- People who teach the untutored, who care for the sick, or who preach the gospel are to be admired. But service to God's world is not confined to those who, as the expression goes, work for the good of humanity. How well one works, how one seeks just relationships at work and what one does with one's work generally defines the value of work.

- God's kingdom advances incrementally. Workaday Christians need not apologize for the small steps they take toward advancing peace, alleviating poverty and enhancing human dignity. Peace Corps volunteers and the like certainly promote the kingdom of God, but so do conscientious carpenters, homemakers, artists, executives, janitors and editors.

- Full-time work on behalf of social justice, for example as a Church employee, contributes to the transformation of society. Even more important and necessary, however, is the role of committed women and men giving flesh to gospel values from inside their workplaces, businesses, schools and communities.

PRINCIPLE #8: ON THE SEVENTH DAY

More than ever before, the people of God must live by the injunction "Keep holy the Sabbath."

IMPLICATIONS:

- An economy which encourages workaholics is no friend to lay spirituality. Our economy and culture need to recognize that holiness (wholeness) for everyday Christians and others in a post-industrial society should include a Sabbath day each week, some Sabbath minutes each day and, optimally, a Sabbath retreat once a year.

- Volunteering in parish and neighborhood organizations is commendable, but the most responsible activity for a busy Christian on a given evening or Saturday morning may well be to nourish his or her family life, intellectual life or cultural life.

• A living wage is every person's birthright, but so too is music, literature and beauty. Christians must, as Vatican II says, "become conscious that they are the artisans and authors of the culture in their community" and thus strive to nurture the best in the arts and society.

PRINCIPLE #9: THE LAITY'S MISSION

The mission to bring about God's kingdom on earth as it is in heaven belongs to every baptized person. Pastoral activity should support that primary mission.

IMPLICATIONS:

• The laity are the church in the heart of the world and bring the heart of the church to the world. Bishops and priests represent Christ in their pastoral ministry which supports and challenges all Christians to represent Christ in their work in the world.

• The word vocation and attention to the vocation crisis should not be restricted by anyone in the church to the ordained priesthood, the permanent diaconate or vowed religious life. There is a vocation shortage of committed citizens, of responsible fathers and others. There are vocation crises in parenting, in nursing and elsewhere.

• Parishes, Newman Centers, and Church agencies need to evaluate all their programs in the context of how well those programs train and support the laity to live their baptism on the job, around the home and in the neighborhood. All of the courses and programs used to train the laity for ministry—either as volunteers or as professional lay ministers—need to be evaluated against their effectiveness in focusing the lay ministers on the crucial task of inspiring people for their work in the world.

AFTERWORD
by William Droel

I moved to Chicago (the city of neighborhoods) in the 1970s, attracted by its reputation for Catholic social action and its fascinating fabric of ethnicity and race.

Within blocks of my Southwest side apartment in those days I found five Catholic churches, each with a grammar school. There was also a Russian Orthodox church, a half dozen Protestant churches, one synagogue serving two congregations and one storefront mosque. There was a Knights of Columbus hall, a VFW hall and three ethnic clubs. There was a YMCA, a cultural center, two city libraries, two public grammar schools, a large public high school, a private high school, a motherhouse, the headquarters of a religious order, a Catholic hospital, a small union hall, a religious shrine with gift shop, and the joint offices for two community organizations and a commercial development agency. There was an unemployment office, a public health clinic, the offices of a weekly newspaper, a ward office, a police station, a firehouse, a small Salvation Army shelter and a small facility for the hearing impaired. And, of course, there was a tavern on every corner, each populated by its regulars.

This was not unusual for Chicago at that time. I found a whole new set of similar institutions when, with my bride, I later moved seven blocks north and four blocks west of my first apartment (a.k.a. "the Cool Pad").

Upon my arrival in the Windy City I was enthralled by the Chicago style of journalism and literature that celebrated the urban characters who inhabited its neighborhood haunts. Reporters and columnists and novelists in Chicago customarily told the grand stories of politics and current events through the foibles and small heroics of ordinary working people. There was even a series of mystery stories based in Chicago's Southside, in which the detective solved the crime precisely by using the mediating structures of parish and precinct.

But things were changing—both in my neighborhood and in our country's social fabric. Sociologists began noting a decline in membership in churches, labor unions and more. In fact, one book—*The Lost City* by Alan Ehrenhalt

(Harper Collins, 1996)—used my neighborhood as a case study for the decline of social capital.

The decline of an older urban/ethnic kind of community would be less consequential if it were being replaced by new forms of community...in the suburbs or in gentrified city areas, for example. However, our computer-based economy, the mobility of investments and workforce, the speedy cultural assimilation of most immigrants and other factors only add to the precipitous depreciation of social capital across the nation.

Of course, the old urban/ethnic neighborhoods should not be romanticized. But it is hard for me to see that so-called "gated communities" in outlying areas, much less websites like MySpace or Facebook, are adequate replacements for parish societies or bowling leagues.

Robert Putnam of Harvard University has extensively researched the phenomenon of social capital. In his book *Bowling Alone* (Simon & Schuster, 2000) and in follow-up articles, Putnam documents the unrelenting withering of voluntary groups of all kinds. People born after 1930 are, he documents, less and less engaged in community affairs and more distrustful of churches, unions, charitable agencies and the like. A major disengagement by people in all age groups occurred during the 1980s. Even though, for example, the number of bowlers increased from 1980-1993, participation in bowling leagues decreased by 40% over those same 13 years, Putnam finds. People were literally "bowling alone."

Putnam analyzed all possible causes to explain why people in the 21st century are less able or less motivated to participate in church activities, union meetings, ethnic clubs, bowling leagues and the like. While there are "many culprits," he does not find a direct causal line from "the usual suspects" to lower involvement. For example, the increased number of women in the paid labor force might seem like an explanation. Yet women who work outside the home are involved in voluntary associations at a higher rate than their counterparts. While not isolating one catchall cause, Putnam finds many indications of increased individualism among those born after 1930 and particularly those born after 1960.

Putnam does find "one prominent suspect" against whom there is "direct incriminating evidence." A cause-and-effect relationship exists between increased time spent in front of a TV and decreased time spent in community activities.

In one of several surveys, Putnam measures attitudes and behaviors before-and-after the national trauma of September 11, 2001. That murderous attack marks a measurable (and in some cases a surprising) shift in attitudes about security, religious pluralism, immigration and other matters. But most people's lives, Putnam finds, "returned to normal relatively quickly." That is, people went back to watching TV most nights, and this behavioral shift persists: People in the United States have, on average, increased their TV time by 16% and further decreased their volunteer time since September 11th.

Our modern values of democracy, pluralism, individual choice and freedom of lifestyle are major achievements and beneficial to our Catholic faith at its best. However, there is a serious downside to the contemporary American lifestyle. Left unchecked, modern values, especially individualism, corrode communal morality and culture. Without a countervailing philosophy to TV and other purveyors of individualism, today's young adults conclude that the answer to all questions comes out of an individual's own emotions and experience.

Today's extreme individualism is not sufficient for a whole, holy life. Young adults (such as my two college-age kids) need a guiding philosophy, some disciplines and social habits that will reinforce the values of community, solidarity, friendship, commitment, neighborly sacrifice and more. The Catholic Church, with its social thought being constantly challenged and updated by new styles of movements, networks and organizations, is one compelling source of an alternative to the vacuous ideology of individualism.

What young adults often lack are habits of the mind and imagination. They do not have a time-tested philosophy to help them function on the job, around the home and in the wider community. They generally know enough to "do good and shun evil." They have not, however, acquired a way to translate their basic dispositions into a sophisticated analysis that sustains them over the long haul. My students at the community college where I teach and other young adults whom I meet are inundated with factoids, loaded with clichés and busy with many obligations. Yes, they are blessed with opportunity, but they are deprived of meaning. They enjoy many freedoms, but they wander in a teleological desert.

Catholic social thought is precisely about the purpose of life. When presented in a compelling way, it is a collective outlook on ultimate purposes. With its opti-

mistic sacramental imagination and its emphasis on the common good, subsidiarity and other solid principles, Catholic social thought balances the dominance
of the market, the individuating tendency of technology and the harshness of
modern individualism. It puts personal relationships on the top of the agenda.

Young Catholic activists are urgently needed in the world, and I hope reading the words of the people in this book might inspire one or two of you. If you
were to ask my advice, I'd tell you to spend less time on the computer and watching reality shows, and generally less energy on things that don't go very deep. I'd
tell you to come to Chicago and look up Greg Pierce (Northside, Cubs fan) and
me (Southside, White Sox fan), as we looked up Russ Barta and Ed Marciniak
years ago. We'd meet with you for sure and introduce you around to some interesting people. Church, Chicago-style is still very much alive.

Today's activists have to craft an alternative to what columnist Thomas
Friedman calls our "Interruption Age." We have a surfeit of connecting devices,
notably the cell phone, the fax machine and the Internet. Yet we are not connecting. *The American Sociological Review*, for example, reports that in 2005 people
on average could name only two close friends; down from three close friends in
1985. The close friends in 2005 also are more likely to be related than in 1985—
suggesting even more insularity.

Today's activists—Catholics and others—are thus challenged to make a culture of real and sustained connections, with an emphasis on crossing economic,
racial and familial lines. The mission of Christians today, as in the past, is political
and cultural, as well as religious and spiritual. Church, Chicago-style has always
understood this.

Chicago is a great place to "do" church. You are invited to join us anytime, no
matter where you find yourself.

ACKNOWLEDGMENTS

Thanks to Robert Droel for typing this manuscript.

Thanks to Vaile Scott for research assistance and suggestions.

Thanks to Sister Patricia Crowley, OSB, for contributing the Foreword.

Thanks for permission to reprint articles from *America* magazine, the Association of Chicago Priests, Catholic News Service, the National Center for the Laity, *Saint Anthony Messenger* magazine and Mary Irene Zotti.

OTHER BOOKS FROM THE CHURCH IN CHICAGO

Finding My Way in a Grace-Filled World. William Droel tells the story of his move to the Southwest Side of Chicago, his involvement in family, church and community there, 112-page paperback, $9.95

The Mass Is Never Ended: Rediscovering Our Mission to Transform the World. Gregory Pierce gives his best argument for taking the Dismissal from Mass seriously and ties it to our mission to transform the world. 126-page paperback, $10.95

Running into the Arms of God: Stories of Prayer/Prayer as Story. Father Patrick Hannon, CSC, uses the liturgical hours as a frame on which to hang twenty-one stories of prayer in the ordinary events of daily life. 128-page hardcover, $15.95; paperback, $11.95

The Geography of God's Mercy: Stories of Compassion and Forgiveness. Father Patrick Hannon, CSC, dives into the common experiences of life and surfaces with nuggets of spiritual gold that reveal the countless ways God shows unconditional love. 160-page hardcover, $17.95; paperback, $12.95

Spirituality at Work: Ten Ways to Balance Your Life On-the-Job. Gregory Pierce offers ten "disciplines" that can be practiced in virtually every workplace to raise your awareness of the presence of God and to allow that awareness to change how you do your work. 160-page paperback, $14.95

Jesus and His Message: An Introduction to the Good News. Legendary Chicago pastor and missionary to Panama Father Leo Mahon provides a clear picture of Jesus and the times in which he lived and the "kingdom" or "reign" of God that he preached. 110-page paperback, $6.95

Gospel Food for Hungry Christians: Matthew, Mark, Luke, John. Theologian John Shea covers the essence of each of the four Gospels in this popular audio series. Six 60-90 minute compact discs in each of the four separate programs, $29.95 each

Available from Booksellers or call 800-397-2282 www.actapublications.com